J. MARTIN EVANS

The Road from Horton: Looking Backwards in "Lycidas"

E|LS
EDITIONS

ELS Editions
Department of English
University of Victoria
Victoria, BC
Canada V8W 3W1
www.elseditions.com

Founding Editor: Samuel L. Macey

General Editor: Luke Carson

Printed by CreateSpace

English literary studies monograph series
ISSN 0829-7681 ; 28
ISBN-10 0-920604-09-9
ISBN-13 978-0-920604-09-0

CONTENTS

Acknowledgements   5

Introduction   7

CHAPTER ONE   All Their Echoes   9

CHAPTER TWO   Young Lycidas   13

CHAPTER THREE   Yet Once More   19

CHAPTER FOUR   Your Old Bards   24

CHAPTER FIVE   Orpheus   36

CHAPTER SIX   The Thankless Muse   45

CHAPTER SEVEN   The Hungry Sheep   50

CHAPTER EIGHT   Joy and Love   58

CHAPTER NINE   Pastures New   66

Notes   75

ACKNOWLEDGEMENTS

I would like to record my gratitude to: the Oxford University Press for permission to include in chapter four a modified version of my study "Daphnis, Gallus, and Lycidas" which appeared in *Renaissance Studies Presented to Dame Helen Gardner*, ed. John Carey (Oxford: Clarendon Press, 1980); the American Council of Learned Societies for a generous grant-in-aid which permitted me to pursue much of the research for this volume at the Bodleian Library, Oxford; to Stanford University, and in particular to Deans Halsey Royden and Norman Wessells who made available the time and the word-processing equipment which enabled me to bring this study to a timely conclusion; and to my colleagues, Professors John Bender, John Freccero, Donald Howard, Herbert Lindenberger, Ronald Rebholz, David Riggs and Wesley Trimpi, who contributed many useful suggestions and corrections. Any errors that remain are not there for want of their vigilance.

INTRODUCTION

One suggestive metaphor for a developmental crisis is a man alone on a body of water trying to get from Island Past to Island Future. He fears that he will not reach Future. He feels that he can move neither forward nor backward, that he is on the verge of drowning. A man may experience himself as swimming alone, as rowing in a leaky boat, or as captain of a luxurious but defective ship caught in a storm. There are wide variations in the nature of the vehicle, the sources of threat and the nature of Past and Future. The critical thing is that the integrity of the enterprise is in serious doubt: he experiences the imminent danger of chaos, dissolution, the loss of the future.[1]

When he wrote *Lycidas* in 1637 Milton was almost twenty-nine years old. For the past five years he had been living with his parents, first in Hammersmith and later in the rural village of Horton. Deeply committed to the ideals of studious retirement and sexual abstinence, he was unmarried, unemployed, and relatively unknown. His chief ambition was to be a great poet. During the five years following the composition of *Lycidas* he travelled extensively in France and Italy, took up residence in London, married Mary Powell, and established himself as one of the principal public champions of the Puritan and Parliamentarian cause. With the exception of an occasional sonnet, he did not complete another poem in English until he was almost sixty.

This drastic change in the direction of his life suggests that Milton underwent what Daniel J. Levinson has called an Age Thirty Transition, a period of psychological crisis in which one's past is reappraised and one's future redefined. During the Age Thirty Transition, Levinson writes:

the provisional, exploratory quality of the twenties is ending and a man has a sense of greater urgency.... He has the feeling: "If I want to change my life—if there are things in it that I don't like, or things missing that I would like to have—this is the time to make a start, for soon it will be too late." The Age Thirty Transition provides a "second chance" to create a more satisfactory life structure within early adulthood.[2]

My thesis is that *Lycidas* records the beginning of such a transition.

7

Although the interpretation that follows will thus run counter to the prevailing view of *Lycidas* as an impersonal exercise in the conventions of the pastoral elegy, I am not proposing a return to the naively biographical approach of critics like E. M. W. Tillyard and Robert Graves who virtually ignore the poem's relationship to the generic traditions lying behind it. Indeed, I shall argue that it was precisely through his dialogue with the pastoral and elegaic traditions that Milton first came face to face with the frustrations and pressures which were to change the future course of his life.

Nor do I wish to suggest that *Lycidas* is a consciously self-expressive or even a deliberately self-analytical poem. Like so much of Milton's early verse, it is first and foremost an occasional, and to that extent a public, work. Its announced purpose is to mourn the untimely death of Edward King, not to reveal Milton's misgivings about his own career. But beneath the marmoreal formality of the surface, I believe, Milton can be observed in the process of discovering some of his deepest anxieties. The poem is simultaneously a public tribute to a learned friend and an intensely private encounter with the accumulated doubts and fears which would eventually transform the retiring young virgin poet of Horton into the publicly outspoken, thrice married polemicist of Westminster.

CHAPTER ONE

All Their Echoes

In one of the most haunting passages in the poem, Milton describes how the natural landscape reacted to the death of Lycidas:

> But O the heavy change, now thou art gon,
> Now thou art gon, and never must return!
> Thee Shepherd, thee the Woods, and desert Caves,
> With wilde Thyme and the gadding Vine o'regrown,
> And all their echoes mourn. (37-41)[1]

The editors of the *Variorum Commentary* are probably right in detecting a sidelong glance at the myth of Echo and Narcissus in the final phrase,[2] for the "Sweet Queen of Parly," as the Lady calls her in *Comus*,[3] is not only present in the repeated clauses and pronouns of the previous four lines; she presides over the entire poem. For instance, Milton begins his elegy with an echo—"Yet once more, O ye Laurels, and once more . . ." —and then, when the thought of the Christian resurrection leads him to make a fresh start at line 165, he signals his intention by echoing the echo, rhythmically and verbally—"Weep no more, woful Shepherds weep no more." As Josephine Miles has remarked,[4] *Lycidas* is full of such repetitions: "For Lycidas is dead, dead ere his prime, Young Lycidas . . . Begin then, Sisters of the sacred well, . . . Begin . . . Together both . . . and both together . . . The Muse her self that Orpheus bore, The Muse her self . . . Return Alpheus . . . Return Sicilian Muse . . . And now the Sun had stretch'd out all the hills, And now . . ."[5] We might almost be listening to an exercise in the various iterative schemes which the rhetoricians of the period have taught us to recognize. To a still greater degree than Marvell's address to his coy mistress, Milton's tribute to his chaste friend is an "echoing song."[6]

There is also another kind of echo in the passage I quoted above, one that reaches far beyond the immediate confines of the text itself. Early in Virgil's fifth *Eclogue* Mopsus invites Menalcas to observe "how the wild vine with its stray clusters has overrun the cave."[7] Milton virtually translates this description in his account of the "desert Caves" overgrown with "the gadding Vine," thereby inviting us to see behind Edward King the figure of Daphnis, the legendary Greek shepherd whose death is commemorated in the Latin poem. As generations of editors from Thomas Newton to A. S. P. Woodhouse have pointed out, Milton's elegy resonates throughout with such allusions. Beginning with the actual title, direct and indirect references to earlier pastorals combine to create a context so dense with association that in retrospect *Lycidas* appears to be a much larger poem than it really is. As the moments of recognition accumulate, the text gradually expands in our minds until we have the paradoxical sense that it contains the tradition to which it belongs. If pastoral is "the art of the backward glance,"[8] then *Lycidas* represents a vastly magnified example of the genre, offering us as it does not just a backward glance but a comprehensive retrospect.

The experience of reading Milton's tribute to Edward King is thus a good deal more strenuous than that of reading anything else he had written up to this point in his career. We seem to be engaged in an activity which is simultaneously receptive and creative, as if the completed poem were at least partly the product of our literary-historical sensibilities. And so in a way it is, for the chamber in which all the echoes finally congregate is the reader's harmonizing memory.

In substantive as well as in formal terms, then, repetition is of the very essence in this work. Everything in *Lycidas*, one could say without too much exaggeration, happens twice—including the repetitions themselves, which often turn out to be echoes of echoes, as in the case of line 165, or allusions to allusions, as in the case of the address to the nymphs.[9] Indeed the entire poem is a kind of recurrence: "Yet once more . . ."[10]

This phenomenon is hardly surprising when we recall how deeply the idea of repetition was ingrained in the cultural consciousness of the Renaissance. The period as a whole defined itself as a revival of an earlier civilization, and this self-perception was reflected in turn by the basic imperative of the educational system: the imitation of the ancients. As a product of that system, Milton not only revitalized the major classical genres; he seems at times to have thought of himself as reliving the actual experience of the classical authors.

As these examples suggest, however, repetitions are rarely, if ever, exact, particularly literary ones. For by virtue of the simple fact that they occur in new contexts, restatements inevitably modify their originals in one way or another. The second time is never quite the same as the first. In the case of biblical typology, for instance, the Old Testament figures are completed rather than merely duplicated by their New Testament fulfilments. In *Paradise Regained* the second Adam thus initiates the redemption of the human race by living out in the Galilean wilderness a perfected version of the first Adam's sojourn in the garden of Eden. "For as by one man's disobedience many were made sinners; so by the obedience of one shall many be made righteous."[11] So superior was the fulfilment to its figure, indeed, that the relationship between the two was frequently assumed to be essentially antithetical. Opposite the Old Testament types stood the New Testament antitypes. Nor was this contrastive approach confined to the interpretation of the bible. The legends of classical Greece and Rome, too, could be read as reverse images of scriptural truths, pagan fictions destined to be corrected by Christian facts. For the Christian humanists of the Renaissance, the Virgin Mary was an antitype not only of Eve but of Venus.

In much the same way the recurrences in *Lycidas* often turn out to be inversions rather than reiterations of their antecedents. The weary "once more" of the first line gives way to a triumphant "no more" as Milton announces King's resurrection. "For Lycidas is dead" (8) is eventually cancelled by "For Lycidas your sorrow is not dead" (166), while the twice repeated downward movement of "sunk so low" (102) and "Sunk though he be" (167) suddenly turns upward with the concluding assertion that the dead shepherd is "sunk low, but mounted high" (172). Like true mirror images, the internal echoes in *Lycidas* transpose what they reproduce. In a world containing "blind mouths" (119), the logic of the poem persuades us, it is only natural that there should also be eyes that "suck" (140).[12]

The same basic pattern is also observable in the way the external echoes operate. J. A. Wittreich's comment on the poem's relation to the other elegies in *Justa Edouardo King Naufrago* accurately describes its relation to the entire pastoral tradition as well. "Nearly every point of contact," he states, "upon scrutiny, becomes a point of contrast."[13] Over and over again what strikes us is not so much the appropriateness as the glaring inappropriateness of Milton's allusions to the works of his predecessors. The more we learn about the various figures the poet marshalls for comparison with Edward King, the less they appear to resemble him. Lycidas himself, as we shall see in Chapter 2, was usually the mourner in pastoral elegies; here he is the deceased. Daphnis, whose ghost accompanies Lycidas throughout the poem, was a famous lover; his seventeenth-century counterpart dies chaste. And Orpheus, King's mythic surrogate in the poem, was murdered by the Bacchantes; Milton's "hapless youth" dies by accident. Each *déjà vue* thus proves to be on closer inspection a

11

vue renversée. We are being persuaded by the poem's allusive strategy to look backwards in more senses than one.

My chief contention in the following pages will be that reversal is the basic structural principle at work in *Lycidas*, that the casual antimetabole with which the poet identifies himself with his subject—"Together both . . . and both together"—enacts in miniature the strategy of the entire poem. Thematically, as Richard P. Adams and others have demonstrated,[14] the elegy develops an elaborate antithesis between the concepts of death and rebirth. Generically, as I shall argue in chapter 4, *Lycidas* illustrates Harold Bloom's dictum that "poetic influence—when it involves two strong, authentic poets,—always proceeds by a misreading of the prior poet, an act of creative correction that is actually and necessarily a misinterpretation."[15] Milton's poem seems to have been written *against* the tradition of the pastoral elegy, *contra* such poems as Theocritus' first *Idyl* and Virgil's tenth *Eclogue*. And psychologically, as I argue in the concluding chapters, *Lycidas* marks a crucial *peripeteia* in Milton's own career, signalling a major reversal in his values and in the subsequent course of his life. Despite its rejection of "denial" (18), *Lycidas* is one long act of contradiction.

CHAPTER TWO

Young Lycidas

The seventeenth century took the business of titles seriously, and not just the aristocratic kind—witness Milton's *Sonnet XI*. So when a contemporary reader came to the final poem in *Justa Edouardo King Naufrago*, the first question to arise might well have been: why *Lycidas*? The opening lines would immediately have supplied a partial answer: because the name is redolent of pastoral, and Milton's contribution to the volume, unlike the others, is a pastoral elegy. But although this narrows the question, it does not dispose of it, for one could still ask with Louis L. Martz: "why, of all the pastoral names available, should Milton have chosen that one name Lycidas?"[1] According to the editors of the *Variorum Commentary* "there seems to be no special significance in the choice,"[2] and indeed, to the best of my knowledge, Martz's is the only serious attempt to discover any.[3] Yet Milton was not in the habit of naming his works arbitrarily. We know from the evidence of the drafts in the Trinity Manuscript that he considered at least three possible titles for *Paradise Lost* before settling upon his original version. If he chose to call Edward King by one pastoral pseudonym rather than another, he is likely to have had a good reason for doing so.

The task of discovering that reason is complicated by the sheer popularity of the particular pseudonym he selected. Watson Kirkconnell recently announced that a reading of W. L. Grant's *Neo-Latin Literature and the Pastoral* had yielded no fewer than thirty-two "Lycidas"'s in Latin pastoral alone,[4] and a study of Greek, Italian and English sources would probably add as many instances again. Fortunately, however, Milton himself has provided a clue which may serve to reduce the potential evidence to manageable proportions. In his very next elegy, the *Epitaphium Damonis*, he describes his visit to Florence in the following terms:

> Oh, how wondrous great was I, when, stretched at ease by the prattlings of the cool Arno, in its poplar grove, where the grass was softest, I could pluck now violets, now the tips of the myrtles, and could hear Menalcas vying with Lycidas! (129-32)

13

The reference to competition points towards Theocritus' seventh *Idyl* in which a goatherd called Lycidas engages in a singing match with Simichidas. The identification of his competitor as Menalcas, on the other hand, recalls Virgil's ninth *Eclogue* in which Lycidas, now a shepherd, discusses with Moeris the poetic achievement of a friend bearing that name.[5] It was these two poems, I believe, that Milton intended his audience to bring to mind when he called his earlier elegy *Lycidas*.

Milton's simultaneous allusion to them in the *Epitaphium Damonis* is not, of course, the only connection between the seventh *Idyl* and the ninth *Eclogue*. As Michael C. J. Putnam has emphasized,[6] the Latin work closely resembles the Greek in setting if not in theme. For instance, although neither of them is an elegy, they both take place in the immediate vicinity of a grave. When Simichidas meets Lycidas at the beginning of the *Idyl* he is almost within sight of the tomb at Brasilas, and when Lycidas and Moeris finish their conversation in the *Eclogue* the tomb of Bianor is just coming into view. We are just one step removed from the situation in Poussin's *Et in Arcadia ego* or the scene which Milton wistfully conjures up in *Lycidas*:

> So may some gentle Muse
> With lucky words favour my destin'd Urn,
> And as he passes turn,
> And bid fair peace be to my sable shrowd. (19-22)

Nor is this the only similarity between the two classical poems. In both, the encounter with Lycidas occurs in the middle of a journey. Theocritus' characters are *en route* from the city to the country, Virgil's from the country to the city. For the duration of their respective dialogues, they are suspended in a kind of metaphorical no-man's-land between the urban and the pastoral worlds. As a result, one has a strong sense of hiatus, of arrested movement, as if the poems themselves were interruptions in a process of transition which cannot be completed until they are over. Milton's *Lycidas*, I shall argue, occupies a very similar position in his personal journey along the road from Horton to Westminster.

Taken individually, the *Idyl* and the *Eclogue* bear still more directly on Milton's elegy. To begin with the former, what makes it so specifically relevant is the actual song that Lycidas offers as his entry in the contest with Simichidas. It is worth quoting at length:

Ageanax will have a fair voyage to Mitylene, even when the Kids are in the west and the south wind drives the wet waves and when Orion holds his feet on the ocean, if he will but set free Lycidas, who is burned by Aphrodite, since a hot love for him consumes me. The halcyons will still the waves, and the sea and the south wind and the east wind, which stirs the seaweed on the highest shore—the halcyons, which are of all birds most beloved by the sea-green Nereids, of all those birds which take their prey from the sea. As Ageanax makes his voyage to Mitylene, may all be favourable to him, and may he reach harbour after a happy journey. On that day I will crown my head with a wreath of dill or of roses or even of gillyflowers, and I will draw the wine of Ptelea from the bowl as I recline by the fire and someone shall roast the bean on the fire. And my couch shall be elbow-deep, thickly covered with fleabane and asphodel and curling celery. And lying at ease, I will drink, calling Ageanax to mind in my very cups and pressing my lips to the dregs. Two shepherds shall play the pipe for me, one from Archarnae and one from Lycope, while Tityrus shall sing close by how once Daphnis, the cowherd, loved Xenea and how the mountain was sorely afflicted about him and how the oaks mourned for him, the oaks that grow by the banks of the river Himera, when he wasted away as the snow melts beneath the lofty Haemus or Athos or Rhodope or remotest Caucusus. (52-77)[7]

The irony of naming "a learned Friend, unfortunately drown'd in his passage from Chester on the Irish Seas," after a shepherd who bade his lover a safe voyage across the Aegean is too exact to be accidental. It is reinforced, moreover, by the two Renaissance elegies most closely resembling Milton's, Jacob Sannazaro's *Phyllis* (1526), in which Lycidas is a fisherman bewailing the death of a young woman he loved, and Giles Fletcher the Elder's *Adonis* (1576), in which he is a spokesman for the poet mourning the death of Clere Haddon, who was drowned in the Cam.[8] Once again the roles are reversed in *Lycidas.* The figure who stood weeping on the seashore or the riverbank is now buried under the "whelming tide" (157), himself the occasion for an elegy.

But the song in the seventh *Idyl* is the source of two additional ironies which cut still deeper. First, even though he did not "reach harbour after a happy journey," Milton's Lycidas nevertheless enjoys a celestial version of the pastoral delights that his predecessor had anticipated for himself upon Ageanax' safe arrival:

> So Lycidas sunk low, but mounted high,
> Through the dear might of him that walk'd the waves,
> Where other groves, and other streams along,
> With Nectar pure his oozy Locks he laves,
> And hears the unexpressive nuptial Song,
> In the blest Kingdoms meek of joy and love.

15

>There entertain him all the Saints above,
>That sing, and singing in their glory move,
>And wipe the tears for ever from his eyes. (172-81)

What Gilbert Lawall has called "a utopian dream of peace and quiet"[9] in the pagan poem gives way to a paradisal vision of beatitude in its Christian successor. Theocritus' rustic musicians are supplanted by the sweet societies of Puritan saints, and Tityrus' dirge lamenting the love-death of Daphnis is replaced by the anthem celebrating the marriage of the lamb in Revelation. As we shall soon see, there is a special appropriateness about that final substitution, for Daphnis, who also makes a brief appearance in the ninth *Eclogue*, is one of the chief representatives of classical pastoral associated with Edward King in the earlier stages of *Lycidas*. Milton's invocation to the Muses, for instance, is modelled upon the refrain of Theocritus' *Lament for Daphnis*—"Begin, dear Muses, begin the pastoral song"[10] (64). Second, even though he undergoes the very fate from which his counterpart in the *Idyl* wished to protect Ageanax, Milton's Lycidas finally proves to be a "Genius of the shore" after all, guarding not just one traveller but "all that wander in that perilous flood" (183-85).

We never find out whether Lycidas' protective song in the *Idyl* has had the desired effect, but the relaxed and light-hearted tone of the work as a whole suggests that Ageanax did indeed arrive safely at his destination. In Virgil's ninth *Eclogue*, on the contrary, the power of poetry to shape events is called into serious question. Commenting on Lycidas' opening speech in that poem, Putnam writes: "If chance overturns all things . . . will the poet's song have the ability to reverse the workings of fortune and save everything? Can poetry, intimate and crucial part of bucolic life that it is, preserve it from destruction?"[11] Virgil's answer, as he goes on to argue, is a qualified "no." At first, Lycidas is surprised by the news that Moeris has been expelled from his lands; he had heard a rumour that "your Menalcas had with his songs saved all" (10). But Moeris quickly disabuses him of any such fanciful notions: "You had heard, and so the story ran," he replies "but amid the weapons of war, Lycidas, our songs avail as much as, they say, the doves of Chaonia when the eagle comes" (11-12). Together the two shepherds then attempt to recall some of their favourite songs, only to discover that they can no longer recollect them in their entirety. "The measure I remember," remarks Lycidas as he tries to recite Moeris' apostrophe to Daphnis, "could I but keep the words" (45). Moeris' reply anticipates the "mere oblivion" of Melancholy Jaques' portrayal of old age. "Time robs us of all, even of memory," he declares. "Now I have forgotten all my songs. Even voice itself now fails Moeris" (51-54). Death is clearly not far off, and it is no accident that in the next speech Lycidas announces that they are arriving at a tomb.

The contrast with the *Idyl* is striking. Gone is the buoyant optimism of Theocritus' characters, and with it their confidence in the efficacy of their own poetic talents. When Simichidas proclaimed that:

> I too am a clear-voiced mouthpiece of the Muses and all call me the best of singers. But I do not readily believe them, by Zeus, for to my thinking I do not yet surpass either that excellect Sicelidas of Samos or Philitas in singing, but I would contend against them as a frog against the locusts (37-41)

it was simply a ruse to induce Lycidas to perform his song first. But when Virgil's Lycidas states that:

> Me, too, the Pierian maids have made a poet; I, too, have made songs; me also the shepherds call a bard, but I trust them not. For as yet, me-thinks, I sing nothing worthy of a Varius or a Cinna, but cackle as a goose among melodious swans (32-36)

there is no reason to believe that he is being anything but sincere. He and Moeris are no Vladimir and Estragon—the master they are waiting for really exists—but the setting in which Virgil has placed them is almost as inimical to the human imagination as the desolate world of Beckett's play. As Putnam has said, "*Idyl* 7 is a poem about joy in song, about the beauty and variety of poetry, set in the context of a journey to a haven of particular beauty. The ninth *Eclogue* is opposite in tone and meaning. Virgil's road leads not toward the glorious retreat of a harvest festival but out of the country in the direction of the city, through a landscape where song is impossible."[12]

Once again the relevance to Milton's *Lycidas* is subtle but direct. For as I shall show in chapter 7, one of the major issues raised by the death of Edward King has to do with the value of poetry in a society that has been deafened by the "hideous roar" (61) of Bacchic revellers or corrupted by the "lean and flashy songs" (123) of faithless shepherds. Writing in the aftermath of a civil war which had deprived him of his farm, Virgil had pondered the worth of the poetic vocation. Writing during the prelude to a civil war that was to absorb most of his energies for the following decade, Milton is faced with the same question. If the muse is not only thankless but powerless to boot, then what is the point

17

of serving her so strictly? If songs are of no avail among the weapons of war, then what is the point of singing them? For Milton's classically trained audience, then, the mere title of *Lycidas* would have been enough to evoke a whole complex of ideas and associations which look forward to some of the central themes in the body of the poem. In the following chapters I shall explore the most important of them.

CHAPTER THREE

Yet Once More

A reader whose memory of classical pastoral had already been triggered by the title of *Lycidas* would have been unlikely to miss the allusion to Virgil's second *Eclogue* in the opening lines. "You too, O laurels, I will pluck, and you their neighbour myrtle" (54) Corydon had sung in the classical poem as he catalogued the delights he was amassing for his beloved Alexis. Milton's adaptation differs in four significant ways. To begin with, his phraseology suggests, as Virgil's does not, repeated assaults on the berries. "Yet once more" implies "many times before," a whole series of similar occasions in the past. What, then, were they? Not surely, his previous elegies, the last of which had been written in 1631. "Yet" suggests a more recent event than that, as if this present disturbance of the laurel and the myrtle followed hard on the heels of the others. In which case the reference can only be to *Comus*, which Milton had composed in 1634, revised extensively in the following three years, and published, with an epigraph drawn from the very same *Eclogue* he alludes to here, in 1637.

Since he himself evidently had them in mind as he started work on *Lycidas*, these revisions may well have some bearing on its meaning. Apart from a few minor changes in wording, they consisted essentially in the addition of three new passages, namely Comus' suggestion that the Lady stop being so cruel to herself "and to those dainty limms which nature lent For gentle usage, and soft delicacy" (679-80), the Lady's defence of "the sage And serious doctrine of Virginity" (785-86), and the Attendant Spirit's account of the union of Venus and Adonis in the garden of the Hesperides and the ecstasy of Cupid and Psyche in the celestial paradise (999-1010). It is no accident, I shall suggest later, that the lines Milton recalled as he began to compose his tribute to Edward King should have been so deeply concerned with the issue of sexuality.

The second difference between Corydon's and Milton's promises to pluck the laurel and the myrtle is the latter's inclusion of the ivy. In an appendix to his study of "The Owl's Ivy and the Poet's Bays," J. B. Trapp has argued that Milton may have been thinking of the coronations of Mussato in 1315 and Petrarch in 1341, both of which involved all

19

three plants. "The three crowns used in the coronation [of Petrarch]," he writes, "were of ivy because it was thus that Bacchus crowned the first poet; of bay because that tree is for victors, and because poets of ancient times used to hold contests after which the winner was crowned like a victorious general. . . . Myrtle is for Venus . . . because poets are extra-ordinarily amorous and delight to sing the praises of love."[1] Although it seems to me improbable that a reference, however oblique, to the tri-umphal crowning of a live poet could possibly have been intended at this point of *Lycidas*, the traditional association of the laurel with Apollo, the myrtle with Venus, and the ivy with Bacchus is almost certainly operative in the opening lines. As Trapp points out, the connections between the three plants and their respective deities are amply docu-mented in classical and neo-classical literature, and Milton seems to take them virtually for granted in several of his other works.[2]

But if this is the case it is surely somewhat surprising that he should have begun an elegy for a chaste and presumably abstemious young candidate for the priesthood with a reference to Venus' myrtle and Bacchus' ivy. The presence of the latter may perhaps be explained by Horace's use of it in the *Odes* as a reward for learning[3] (the headnote to the 1645 edition of *Lycidas* describes King as "a learned Friend" and Edward Phillips emphasizes his "great learning" in his *Life of Milton*)[4] but there is no getting around the erotic associations of what Milton was to call a few years later "the Paphian myrtle."[5] Newton's old theory that it might have been included because King was "of a proper age for love"[6] has recently been dismissed by the editors of the *Variorum Com-mentary* as "incongruous," though they go on to admit the possibility of "an allusion to some attachment, now unknown."[7] I would like to suggest, on the contrary, that Newton's observation might not have been too wide of the mark. For it is hardly necessary to suppose the existence of some unknown attachment in order to recognize that the goddess of love might have a significant role to play in a poem about an unmarried young man of twenty-five. The original line in Virgil's second *Eclogue* occurred, after all, in a context redolent with sexuality, and, as we have just seen, Milton's rephrasing of it implies that he was remembering his own recent treatment of the subject in *Comus*. Rather than regarding the reference to the myrtle as a mere anomaly, therefore, I think we should be willing to concede that Venus and all she stands for might prove to be a major concern in the rest of the poem.

What is true of the myrtle, moreover, may well be true of the ivy too. For although Bacchus is not physically present in *Lycidas*, as Apollo is, he is never far off stage, and his influence is no less potent in this work than it was in *Comus*. The traditional rival of Apollo, he is indirectly responsible for the death of Orpheus, whose career will subsequently be compared with King's. The traditional ally of Venus, he represents a way of life which, according to the *Elegia Sexta*, is fundamentally opposed to that of the epic poet. In *The Reason of Church Government* Milton thus covenants with his readers to produce one day a work inspired not by Venus or Bacchus—"the heat of youth, or the vapours of wine, like that which flows at wast from the pen of some vulgar Amorist" —but rather by the deity whose spokesman in *Lycidas* is Phoebus Apollo —"that eternall Spirit who can enrich with all utterance and knowledge, and sends out his Seraphim with the hallow'd fire of his Altar to touch and purify the lips of whom he pleases."[8] By listing the laurel, the myrtle, and the ivy in the opening lines of his elegy, Milton is emblematically invoking the three deities between whom he must, like Paris, finally adjudicate.

The third change he made in his classical model concerns the maturity of the berries he proposes to pluck. In Virgil's *Eclogue* there is not the slightest hint that they may be unripe, whereas in *Lycidas* they are "harsh and crude" (3). As Cleanth Brooks and John Hardy have pointed out in their influential commentary, this modification implies an interesting correspondence between the theme of Milton's immature literary talent and the theme of King's premature death. "The poet is unripe," they observe, "but Lycidas, 'dead ere his prime,' Lycidas for whom the berries are to be plucked, was also unripe, untimely dead; and there is therefore an ironic justification in the poet's being compelled to sing thus prematurely."[9] In my view, the analogy has rather more complex and disturbing implications than that, for Milton is in effect doing to his own poetic inspiration what the blind Fury did to Edward King; his "forc'd fingers rude" (4) are performing essentially the same operation as her "abhorred shears" (75), namely cropping the fruit "before the mellowing year" (5). So the act of writing the poem becomes the equivalent of killing its subject all over again. No wonder Milton is so reluctant to begin it.

Which brings us to the fourth and perhaps most profound difference between the address to the evergreens in the classical *Eclogue* and in the seventeenth-century elegy. The latter's weary exordium—Hal would never have said "Yet once more unto the breach"—bespeaks a mood of anguished reluctance which has absolutely no precedent in the sprightly rhythms of Virgil's Latin: "et vos, o lauri, carpam et te, proxima myrte."

21

Milton is clearly averse from gathering the laurel and the myrtle, and his aversion is the dominant emotion in the early part of the poem. As Donald M. Friedman has put it in a recent essay, "the address to the emblematic, honorific plants combines reverent apology and a grinding, reluctant distaste for his enforced task."[10] The composition of *Lycidas*, in fact, constitutes a violation of Milton's poetic integrity, an appalling duty which he had undertaken only because "Bitter constraint, and sad occasion dear, / Compells me to disturb your season due" (6-7).

There is more to this disavowal, I would submit, than the kind of routine coyness that was expected of any Renaissance gentleman who ventured into print. Milton's reticence sounds too genuine to be a conventional exercise in literary *sprezzatura*. One feels it, for instance, in the laboured rhythm of the first two lines, in the allusion to a famous phrase of another reluctant elegist, and in the repeated appeal to the muses to "begin." But most of all one feels it in the persistent, almost compulsive, use of periphrasis. Thus Hesperus is "the star that rose, at Ev'ning" (30), the sun is "the day-star" (168), Sirius is "the swart Star" (138), the muses are the "Sisters of the sacred well" (15), Orpheus is the Muse's "inchanting son" (59), the Bacchantes are "the rout that made the hideous roar" (61), Atropos is "the blind Fury" (75), Triton is "the Herald of the Sea" (89), St. Peter is "the Pilot of the Galilean lake" (109), Christ is "him that walk'd the waves" (173), St. Michael's sword is "that two-handed engine at the door" (130), and the hyacinth is "that sanguine flower inscrib'd with woe" (106). Indeed, one of the reasons that *Lycidas* has attracted so much annotation is that it confronts the reader with a series of riddles, each of which must be solved before he can gain admittance to the poem's private centre.

This unwillingness to name things directly is partly responsible, I suspect, for that air of remoteness to which Dr. Johnson objected so vigorously. The usual way of responding to his criticism is to point out that the pastoral convention, which was dead in his day, was alive in Milton's, and that allusions which in the eighteenth century might have seemed remote would have been perfectly familiar in the seventeenth. But in my judgement Johnson's comments cannot be dismissed so easily, for there is in *Lycidas* an unusually profound disjunction between the singer and his song, a prolonged sense of dissociation which reaches its climax in the literal disengagement of the final *ottava rima*. The same reticence which prevented Milton from identifying some of the major forces in his elegy by their proper names is evident, too, in the difficulty he appears to have in facing his subject head on. It takes him thirty-six lines of grammatical obliquity before he can bring himself to address Edward King directly in the second person, and no sooner has he done so than he retreats back into the impersonality of the third person for another hundred lines or so.

Seen in this light, the repetitions I noted in the Introduction begin to take on psychological as well as structural significance, especially those in the opening paragraph:

> For Lycidas is dead, dead ere his prime,
> Young Lycidas, and hath not left his peer:
> Who would not sing for Lycidas? He knew
> Himself to sing ... (8-11)

Milton seems to be trying to flail himself into an appropriately grief-stricken response to King's death, as if he could only work up the necessary degree of emotional energy to compose his tribute by intoning over and over again the name and condition of its subject. Like the opening stanzas of the abortive ode on the Passion, the induction to *Lycidas* is an act of poetic self-laceration. What is more, as I hope to show in the following chapters, the "denial vain, and coy excuse" (18) which made it necessary did not simply disappear once Milton had determined to overcome on this occasion his self-confessed tendency to be "slow and lazy to write."[11] On the contrary, they continued to be a source of anxiety throughout the rest of the poem. In the final analysis, I believe, reluctance of one kind or another is one of Milton's principal concerns in *Lycidas*.

CHAPTER FOUR

Your Old Bards

The reticence I have just been discussing may also be responsible for the difficulty of determining just where the induction ends and the elegy proper begins. Since Milton had to write himself into the poem, as it were, there is no clearly defined moment of decision, no precise juncture at which we can say that the preliminaries are over and the lament has commenced. Instead, we have a series of false starts, culminating in the address to the nymphs:

> Where were ye Nymphs when the remorseless deep
> Clos'd o're the head of your lov'd Lycidas?
> For neither were ye playing on the steep,
> Where your old Bards, the famous Druids, ly,
> Nor on the shaggy top of Mona high,
> Nor yet where Deva spreads her wisard stream. (50-55)

By the time we reach these lines, most of us would probably agree that the elegy is already under way, yet we may also have the feeling that here if anywhere is its real beginning.[1] For Milton's questions echo those with which the formal lament commences in the two most famous elegies of the entire pastoral tradition, Theocritus' first *Idyl* and Virgil's tenth *Eclogue*:

> Where were you when Daphnis pined away, where were you, O nymphs? Were you in the lovely vales of Peneus or of Pindus? You surely did not haunt the mighty stream of Anapus or the steep of Aetna or the sacred water of Acis. (66-69)

> What groves, what glades were your abode, ye virgin Naiads, when Gallus was pining with a love unrequited? For no heights of Parnassus or of Pindus, no Aonian Aganippe made you tarry. (9-12)

Milton's unusually prolonged and specific imitation of these passages has long been recognized. Indeed, it has been almost too well recognized, for the parallel has become so familiar that it has often been taken for granted. When J. H. Hanford, for example, comes to discuss the relationship between the above-quoted passages in his classic essay on the pastoral elegy, he pauses only to assess the seventeenth-century poet's relative indebtedness to his two classical models. Milton's lines, he concludes, "are directly reminiscent of the Greek rather than the Latin poet."[2] I would suggest, however, that the whole point of the allusion lies in the *doubleness* of its reference. During the previous four verse paragraphs we have caught numerous individual echoes; now, for the space of six lines, we can hear two voices accompanying Milton's in a continuous descant, and our critical energies are more profitably absorbed by the task of exploring the implications of that phenomenon than with worrying about which of the two additional voices sounds the louder.

The phenomenon itself, of course, stems from a simple fact of literary history which most of the poem's audience would have learned at school: Virgil's tenth *Eclogue* is an imitation of Theocritus' first *Idyl*. Moreover, the features which distinguish it as an imitation are precisely those which Milton reproduces, namely the address to the nymphs and the procession of visitors. Like Plato's painted bed in the *Republic*, *Lycidas* may be defined as an imitation of an imitation. In which case Hanford's literary bookkeeping is positively misleading, for if Milton chose to allude to those very elements which the Greek and the Latin poems have in common with each other, one can hardly escape the conclusion that he wanted us to recall both works simultaneously.

As soon as we attempt to do so, however, we encounter a major problem. Despite the verbal and structural similarities between the first *Idyl* and the tenth *Eclogue*, their respective heroes are polar opposites. To begin with the *Idyl*, most recent studies follow G. E. Gebauer in seeing Daphnis as a second Hippolytus who "had vowed to resist love. Aphrodite was affronted and angered by such audacious arrogance and inspired in him an overpowering passion. Rather than gratify it and thereby break his vow, Daphnis chose to languish and die."[3] Following the example of the Greek tragedians, Theocritus dramatizes only the climactic sequence of events, the hero's final decision and subsequent death. The earlier part of the story is gradually reconstructed by the speeches of the minor characters who come, like Samson's visitors, either to divert him from his purpose or to deride him for persisting in it. Each successive encounter sheds fresh light upon the nature of his predicament until, by the time he delivers his parting words, it is fully illuminated.

Thus Hermes' opening question establishes no more than the cause of Daphnis' sickness: "Who makes thee suffer thus? With whom, my good lad, art thou so much in love?" (77-78). Taken on its own, this could well suggest that the lovelorn shepherd was dying of unrequited passion,[4]

25

but Priapus' ensuing rebuke reveals that the situation is more complicated than we might have suspected: "Wretched Daphnis, why doest thou pine away? The maiden is roaming among all the springs, all the groves . . . searching for thee. Thou art too poor a lover and art a helpless creature" (82-85). Clearly Daphnis could indulge his feelings if he wished to, so some further consideration, as yet unspecified, must be holding him back. The jeers of Cypris, who arrives on the scene shortly afterwards, disclose what it is: "Surely thou didst boast, Daphnis, that thou wouldst throw Love for a fall; but hast thou not rather thyself been thrown by irresistible Love?" (97-98). He has evidently taken a vow of chastity, and in revenge Cypris has made him fall in love with the maiden to whom Priapus referred earlier. Only now that his dilemma has been adequately defined does the hero break his silence by announcing his intention to die rather than yield to the power of Cypris. He may be "dragged down to Hades by Love" (130), but even there he promises to "bring grievous pain to Love" (103).

All this, it should be added, represents a radical departure from the more common version of the myth attributed to the two Sicilian poets, Timaeus and Stesichorus, according to which:

> While Daphnis kept cows in Sicily, being very beautiful, a nymph fell in love with him, whom he enjoyed, being in his blooming years. . . . They agreed that he should not enjoy any other, but if he transgressed, she threatened him, that it was deemed by fate that he should lose his sight. . . . Afterwards the King's daughter falling in love with him, he being drunk violated the agreement and lay with her. This was the first occasion of Bucolic verses, the subject whereof was to bewail the misfortune of Daphnis, the loss of his eyes.[5]

Nevertheless, both A. S. F. Gow in his authoritative edition and Gilbert Lawall in his full-length study of the *Idyls* agree with Gebauer that Theocritus completely transformed the traditional version of the story to serve his own purposes. In Lawall's words:

> The nymph of the myth is simply replaced by nature herself. In the myth the nymph made Daphnis swear not to love a woman, but he was finally seduced and punished. Theocritus' Daphnis is made of sterner stuff; a true tragic hero, he resists all temptation and so pines away to his death. By retaining his chastity, he remains faithful to nature, wild animals, woods, and streams.[6]

By no stretch of the imagination could the same claim be made for the famous soldier, statesman and poet, Cornelius Gallus, whose unhappy love affair with Lycoris is the immediate subject of Virgil's tenth *Eclogue*. He is unambiguously and unrepentantly dedicated to sexual passion, and he is dying[7] not because he refuses to indulge his feelings but because he cannot; his mistress has left him for another man. Rejecting all the conventional consolations of pastoral, he continues to love her in spite of her infidelity, and with his last words affirms the sovereignty of Eros: "Love conquers all; let us, too, yield to Love!" (69). The contrast between the Roman warrior and the Greek shepherd could scarcely be more extreme. Daphnis conquered love; Gallus willingly surrenders to it.

As a result, although the processional figures in the *Eclogue* once again reveal the nature of the hero's dilemma, the sentiments they express during the course of their disclosures are far removed from those of their Theocritean predecessors. Whereas Daphnis' visitors came to tempt or to mock him, Gallus' are concerned only to comfort or to admonish him. Priapus, for example, urged Daphnis to pursue his beloved; Apollo advises Gallus to forget her: "Gallus, what madness this? Thy sweetheart Lycoris hath followed another amid snows and amid rugged camps" (22-23). Cypris exulted over the misery of an adversary. Pan tells a fellow-lover to stop grieving: "Will there be no end? . . . Love recks naught of this: neither is cruel Love sated with tears, nor the grass with the rills, nor bees with the clover, nor goats with leaves" (28-30). The theme of the *Idyl* was heroic chastity. The theme of the *Eclogue* is the irresistible power of love.

What, then, are we to make of Lycidas' relationship to the heroes of these two very different poems? Before we can even begin to answer this question, we must first answer a prior one: how were the first *Idyl* and the tenth *Eclogue* interpreted in the sixteenth and early seventeenth centuries? Davis P. Harding and others have taught us that the "Renaissance Ovid" was by no means identical with either the classical or the modern one,[8] and the same is true of the Renaissance Theocritus and the Renaissance Virgil. Certainly, the pastoral works of both were the subject of intense scholarly scrutiny during the hundred or so years preceding the composition of *Lycidas*. The *Idyls* were annotated in considerable detail by such influential humanists as Joseph Scaliger, Isaac Casaubon, Daniel Heinsius,[9] Fredericus Lamotius,[10] and Joannes Meursius.[11] And in order to make them available to a wider audience, Theocritus' works were frequently translated into Latin. By the time Heinsius published his comprehensive collection of Greek bucolic poetry in 1604 no less than six partial or complete Latin versions were already in existence.[12]

Virgil's *Eclogues* were even more exhaustively analyzed. Antonio

27

Mancinelli, Jodocus Badius Ascensius,[13] Joannes Pierius Valerianus, Juan Luis Vives, Helius Eobanus Hessus, Richardus Gorraeus, Philip Melanchthon, Stephanus Riccius, Peter Ramus, and Thomas Farnaby[14] (who, by an odd coincidence, may have been Edward King's teacher)[15] all produced elaborate commentaries, while the annotations of the two best known earlier scholiasts, Servius and Probus, were reprinted throughout the period. In addition, Abraham Fleming,[16] John Brinsley, William Lisle, and John Bidle[17] translated the *Eclogues* into English, often with extensive marginal notes. Brinsley's painstakingly literal version, "written chiefly for the good of schools,"[18] is particularly useful as an indication of the way in which the young Milton may have first encounted the poem. It is with these interpretations of both the first *Idyl* and the tenth *Eclogue* that any discussion of the relationship between *Lycidas* and its models must begin.

One of the first and most interesting facts they reveal is that the differences between the Greek and the Latin poems which I have just discussed appear to have escaped the Renaissance commentators entirely. Melanchthon, Fleming, Brinsley, and Farnaby all emphasized Virgil's debt to Theocritus without so much as a hint that he may have modified his predecessor's meaning in any way. Fleming, for instance, declared in the preface of his translation of the tenth *Eclogue*: "Touching the argument, it is all in a maner taken out of Thirsis, that is, the first Idyl of Theocritus, who handleth the like matter in all points in his Daphnis."[19] In his lecture on Theocritus' first *Idyl* Heinsius claimed that "Virgil translated the most ancient, and to this extent the most original, material of bucolic song [in his poem] to Gallus: the whole of this eclogue. . . . is a kind of imitation of the misfortunes of Daphnis."[20] So closely were the two poems associated with each other, indeed, that they seem to have virtually coalesced in the minds of many sixteenth-century readers.

The most striking evidence of this process is provided by Hessus, who incorporated whole lines from the tenth *Eclogue* into his Latin translation of the first *Idyl*, notably in his rendering of Thyrsis' address to the nymphs:

> Quae nemora, aut qui vos saltus habuere puellae
> Naiades, indigno quum Daphnis amore periret?
> Pulchra ne vos tenuisse putem Peneia Tempe?
> Num iuga Thessalici Phoebo gratissima Pindi?[21]

And when Virgil's *Eclogue* was in turn translated into Greek by Heinsius, Scaliger, and Daniel Alsworth, several of Theocritus' most striking phrases were conscripted into service to Gallus.[22] By the early seventeenth century the first *Idyl* and the tenth *Eclogue* had become almost indistinguishable from each other.

Needless to say, this conflation could not have taken place without a radical transformation in the character of one or other of their respective protagonists. Bearing in mind the chronological priority of the *Idyl*, we might have expected the dissimilarities noted above to have been resolved in favour of Daphnis, but in fact it was Gallus who proved to be the dominant partner. Two factors seem to have been responsible for his victory. First, there was the retrospective influence of the tenth *Eclogue* upon the interpretation of the first *Idyl*. In a critical reversal of the mimetic process of composition, the Greek original was read in the light of the Latin imitation rather than vice-versa, and the chaste pastoral prototype was refashioned in the image of his concupiscent elegiac descendant. Instead of producing the Theocritean Gallus we might have anticipated, the commentators of the sixteenth and seventeenth centuries thus created a distinctly Virgilian Daphnis, animated by the same all-consuming passion that had brought Lycoris' lover to his death. Second, there was the prospective influence, so to speak, of Timaeus' and Stesichorus' version of the myth. For thanks to such references to it as Ovid's in Book IV of the *Metamorphoses*, the notion that Daphnis was an unfaithful lover was still very much alive in the Renaissance. For example, John Rider explained in his etymological dictionary that Daphnis was:

> a young man of Sicily who compacted with a Nymph whom he loved that whether of them soever should violate their faith, which they plighted to one another, should lose both their eyes; Daphnis, forgetting his promise, fell in love with another; the gods that were called to witness in the oath, did punish the breach of it by making him blinde.[23]

In combination these two pressures (the retrospective and the prospective) were irresistible, and Theocritus' defiant virgin reverted to his original amorous *persona*.

The interpretative consequences of these developments are clearly reflected in the commentaries of Lamotius and Heinsius on the first *Idyl*. Both simply took it for granted that Theocritus had followed the traditional form of the Daphnis myth in his treatment of it. As Heinsius wrote:

> Timaeus, the authority on Sicilian matters, calls this nymph Echenais, with whom Daphnis had made an agreement or resolution that he would undergo the penalty threatened by the fates if he broke faith by falling in

love with someone else. . . . Parts of the speeches are assigned to this nymph in the idyl, as will be clear by the emendation of a single word.[24]

The word in question occurs during the course of Priapus' address to the dying shepherd:

> Wretched Daphnis, why doest thou pine away? The maiden is roaming among all the springs, all the groves . . . searching for thee. Thou art too poor a lover and art a helpless creature. (82-85)

The Greek verb rendered here by "searching" is *zateusa*. This, Heinsius ingenuously insisted, made nonsense, for there was no reason that he could see why a maiden who had just been betrayed by her lover should still be searching for him. In place of *zateusa* he therefore proposed another Doric word, *zatosa*, that is, "speaking" or "reproaching." Everything thereafter, he concluded, was spoken not by Priapus as earlier editors had assumed, but by the nymph herself:

> All this speech belongs to the nymph Echenais, who is castigating Daphnis for his promiscuity and unstable raging. By the loves of Theocritus, I swear that there is no passage that has been less understood by the scholiasts and their successors. . . . The Greek scholiast did not see how to resolve these problems, namely how she whom Daphnis had offended could be said to seek him when she ought rather to flee from him. . . . He thinks the whole speech belongs to Priapus who is consoling Daphnis, when in fact it belongs to the indignant girl whom he has betrayed and offended by his inconstancy.[25]

On the basis of this crucial emendation he then went on to summarize the lines I quoted above as follows: "The girl is borne through springs and all the groves and *complains* (*conqueritur*) thus: 'Assuredly, Daphnis, you are too fickle in love and too impetuous.' "[26] So what in the original text had been a light hearted piece of encouragement directed to a steadfast virgin became a deeply felt rebuke delivered by a wronged mistress. Theocritus' innocent shepherd on his way to martyrdom has turned into an unfaithful lover about to pay the just penalty of his transgression.

Virgil's tenth *Eclogue* was treated no less moralistically by the translators and annotators of the period. Servius had remarked in his commentary on the poem that "in Gallus is exhibited the impatience of shameful love [*inpatientia turpis amoris*]."[27] This theme was taken up and developed with evident relish by such Renaissance scholars as Melanchthon, Ramus, Riccius, Farnaby and Brinsley. Although few of them

30

went quite so far as Fleming, who subtitled his translation of the poem "the mad love of Cornelius Gallus,"[28] they all agreed that Virgil's amorous friend was at the very least "fond" as another translator put it.[29] According to Brinsley, for instance, his love for the "harlot" Lycoris was "out of all measure,"[30] and as such it could bring only anguish and degradation in its train. The apparently aimless and disconnected series of fantasies Gallus describes in lines 50-69 revealed, in Riccius' words, the "inconstancy of love [*amoris inconstantiam*],"[31] while the work as a whole revealed the melancholy truth that:

> there is no strength so great, no force of mind so powerful, even in the greatest of men, which cannot be ennervated and dissipated by the entice-ments of love, no vigour so great that it cannot grow languid, cannot be dominated and subjugated by the sweetness of love, which in appearance seems pleasant, delightful and gracious when in reality it is nothing but pure poison [*merum fel*].[32]

But human nature was not entirely at the mercy of Venus and her son. There was, the Renaissance commentators maintained, an external force which could give mankind the strength to resist, namely the agency invoked by Gallus himself at the height of his frenzy:

> I will go, and those verses which I composed in the Chalcidian measure I will now attune to the pipe of the Sicilian shepherd. I am determined to choose suffering in the woods among the dens of wild beasts and to carve the tale of my love in the young trees. (50-54)

In these lines, claimed Brinsley (translating Ramus), "Gallus propounds unto himselfe the remedies which he wil use for the curing of his love, by contrary studies. As first by giving his mind to the studie of Poetrie." Unfortunately, however, he was already too far gone for this classic *remedium amoris* to have any effect. Just twelve lines later, Brinsley went on to note, "the Poet suddenly disliking the former remedies, setteth out the inconstancie of love, and that no remedies can cure it, neither the pleasures of the woods, nor the study of Poetrie, no nor any musicke, nor yet any toyles can asswage the rage thereof."[33] The time for Gallus to have sought the aid of poetry was when he felt the first stirrings of passion.

Which was just the point of Virgil's opening address to the nymphs as the Renaissance commentators interpreted it. As Servius had originally observed,[34] the locations from which the nymphs were absent while Gallus was pining away were all associated with poetic inspiration. Par-nassus and Pindus were both consecrated to Apollo and the Muses, while

Aganippe's literary connections were too well known to deserve comment. The Naiades, it followed, were no other than the Muses, and Virgil's questions to them contained an implicit rebuke to the only power he knew which could have saved his friend from his fate: "He seems to say this," Servius remarked, "because, if the Muses had been present with [Gallus], that is, if he had given [himself] the task of writing songs, he would not have fallen into such amatory difficulties [*tantas amoris angustias*]."[35] In a detailed note on the same passage, Ascensius explained to his Renaissance readers the assumption underlying Servius' interpretation. "The presence of the Muses can restrain love," he pointed out, "because, as the divine poet teaches in Book II of the *Aeneid*, the chaste goddesses have no dealings with Venus, whence Aeneas could not see them until Venus went away." The Naiades were "the goddesses of the fountains, that is, the Muses who preside over the fountains; for according to Varro the Muses and the Nymphs are the same, maidens, that is, chaste and flourishing in perpetual virginity (whence, as Catullus said, the poet ought himself to be chaste). . . . "[36]

By the time Brinsley produced his annotated translation of the *Eclogues* in 1620 this view of the episode was commonplace: "He accuseth the Muses that they were so carelesse of Gallus," he wrote, "to let him so to leave his studies and to perish in such unbeseeming love."[37] Like the fourth book of the *Aeneid*, then, the tenth *Eclogue* was read in the Renaissance as an example of the distracting power of love:

> So love disturbs many from their mind and sanity, and drives them either to say or to do something against the decorum of their persons. For love is a violent fire with which as long as the mind burns, it can restrain itself only with difficulty from breaking bounds. So in this *Eclogue* is set forth the picture of a foolish love [*stulti amatoris imago*] so that by looking at this picture we may learn to avoid all the occasions and enticements by which this fire is wont to be aroused.[38]

"Omnia vincit Amor" was a warning, not an affirmation.

For commentators like Vives and his English translator Lisle this was all far too literalistic. "The matter itselfe and subject of this work," they declared, "doth plainly witnesse in sundry places, that it is not simply, but figuratively spoken, under a shadow: which makes me admire more at Servius Honoratus, who will in this book admit of no Allegories."[39] The dig at Servius was doubly unfair, for not only *did* he admit of allegories, both in theory and in practice,[40] but he unwittingly provided

Vives with the raw material for his figurative interpretation of the tenth *Eclogue* by identifying its subject as follows:

> Cornelius Gallus, the first governor of Egypt . . . was originally a friend of Caesar Augustus; later, when he had come under suspicion of conspiring against Caesar, he was killed.[41]

In Vives' *Interpretatio in Bucolica Vergilii, Potissimum Allegorica* (1539) this brief biographical sketch was transformed into the "Argument" of the entire poem:

> Cornelius Gallus, (a man of most exquisite and dextrous witt, and an admirable Poet, after hee had been preferd to Augustus and rais'd by him to the government of Ægypt), was accused to Caesar, to have conspir'd, and to have attempted something contrary to his mind; for grief of which accusation, hee killed himselfe: This his death Virgil deplores under the title of Love.[42]

Political rather than erotic entanglements were thus responsible for Gallus' downfall, and Virgil's real purpose in writing the elegy was to vindicate a brilliant young statesman whose career had been cut short by the slanderous accusations of his rivals and the gullibility of his emperor. The latter, cast somewhat disconcertingly as Lycoris,[43] had adopted Mark Antony as his new favourite, leaving the hapless governor of Egypt to meditate on the perils of high office.

According to this reading of the poem, then, the address to the nymphs was a rebuke to the muses not for letting Gallus fall in love but for allowing him to be ensnared by affairs of state:

> These were the places of *Gallus* his retrait amongst the Muses, and to the study of sweete Poesie: wherein if hee had still retir'd himselfe, and had not aspired to the great Imployments, and Business of state, which caus'd his ruin, hee had still liv'd.[44]

Unfortunately, like his literal counterpart in Brinsley's commentary, he learned his lesson too late. "I wish now," he lamented in Vives' paraphrase of lines 35-36, "that I had continued my study, amongst my Books, and held mee to my private life, then I had proved learned like others; at least I might have had the happiness, to have been always in the company of Schollars and learned men."[45] The love which had brought about his downfall, the love which Pan insisted could never be "reconciled, or satisfied, with teares, and repentance" was the "love of rule and dominion."[46] "Omnia vincit Amor" was still a warning, but it was a warning against the thirst for power—hence Riccius' rendering of this famous phrase in his *Ecphrasis Allegorica in Decimam Eclogam*: "For nothing will be able to assuage this desire of Augustus for ruling."[47] As Melanchthon put it in one of his comparatively rare excursions into allegory, the hero of the tenth *Eclogue* was "a memorable example of the kind of fortune one gets at court [*memorabile exemplum aulicae fortunae*]."[48]

Seen in this context, as I believe it should be, *Lycidas* begins to look rather less conventional than most critics have taken it to be. Far from being just another pastoral hero who died young, Edward King emerges as the exact antithesis of Daphnis and Gallus, or, more precisely, of the Renaissance Daphnis and Gallus. Unlike both, he had remained chaste all his life, thereby earning the right, reserved for those who "were not defiled with women," of participating in the marriage of the Lamb.[49] His only mistress was his muse. Unlike Daphnis, moreover, he did not betray her. Even though she had proved to be as "thankless" (66) as the cruel and fair lady of the courtly tradition, he resisted the consolations of the nymphs. Amaryllis and Neaera were never able to make him break his vow "to scorn delights, and live laborious dayes" (72). Unlike Gallus, on the other hand, he did not abandon his studies in order to pursue a political career. Nor was he ever suspected of disloyalty to the master he *had* chosen to serve; the bark was "perfidious" (100), not Lycidas. He had meditated his Maker no less "strictly" (66) than his Muse.

We might well conclude, then, that Daphnis and Gallus function in this poem in much the same way that Achilles and Ulysses function in *Paradise Lost*: as counterfigures, whose pagan imperfections define the Christian virtue of Milton's hero. But I believe that there may be rather more to the matter than that. For there is one final difference between Edward King and his two classical predecessors which totally transforms the significance of all the rest: his death was an accident. It simply could not be attributed, as theirs had been, to some fatal error on his part. He had neither sported in the shade nor striven in the field; he had neither fallen in love nor succumbed to the lures of the court. On the contrary, he had obeyed all the rules which the protagonists of the *Idyl* and the *Eclogue* had broken, yet he had still been cut off "ere his prime"(8). Hence the bitterness of Milton's criticism of his own version of the address to the nymphs: "Ay me, I fondly dream! Had ye bin there—for what could that have don?" (56-57). Hence, too, the ensuing allusion to Orpheus' solitary period of abstinence after the death of Eurydice. If a life of austere dedication to poetry was no guarantee of survival, if the "blind Fury" (75) was as powerful and remorseless as Venus and Caesar

Augustus, then what *was* the point of sexual and political self-denial, what *did* it "boot" to "tend the homely slighted Shepherds trade" (64-65)?

The contrasts I have noted between Daphnis and Gallus on the one hand and Edward King on the other could hardly have afforded Milton much comfort, then. They may have demonstrated King's superiority over his predecessors, but they must also have called into question the very standards by which that superiority was measured. The primary allusive context within which Milton chose to lament the fate of his fellow student, I would therefore suggest, may have served to trigger his anxieties not about the possibility of his own premature death, as Tillyard has suggested, but rather about the validity of the "fugitive and cloistered virtue" advocated by the commentators on Theocritus and Virgil, and, still more to the point, the validity of the kind of life he himself had been leading since he had retired to his father's rural estate at Horton. In Boccaccio's *Life of Dante*, which he had recently been reading, the poet's downfall was attributed to his involvement in the political and amorous affairs of Florence. The fate of Edward King, however, seemed to suggest that Boccaccio had overestimated the efficacy of chastity and retirement. Perhaps there was something to be said for the active life of sexual and political engagement after all.

CHAPTER FIVE

Orpheus

Neither Daphnis nor Gallus, of course, is actually mentioned by name in *Lycidas*[1] (though for someone of Milton's etymological sensibilities the tradition linking the former with the Greek word for laurel[2] may well have hinted at an allusion in the opening line). Like Venus and Bacchus, they are invisible but felt presences in the poem's associative hinterland. The anxieties which the Renaissance interpretation of their stories must have aroused in Milton at this particular point of his career could not, however, be left in the background with them. His doubts about the efficacy of chastity and retirement needed an immediate and effective outlet if they were not to undermine the remainder of the elegy. They found it in the figure whose death Milton recalls in the very next lines:

> Ay me, I fondly dream!
> Had ye bin there—for what could that have don?
> What could the Muse her self that Orpheus bore,
> The Muse her self, for her inchanting son
> Whom Universal nature did lament
> When by the rout that made the hideous roar,
> His goary visage down the stream was sent,
> Down the swift Hebrus to the Lesbian shore. (56-63)

In a pioneering article published in 1949 Caroline W. Mayerson declared that this allusion was a "lost metaphor."[3] One could hardly make the same claim today. Detailed investigations by such scholars as Thomas H. Cain, C. Davidson, J. B. Friedman, John Hollander, Joseph Kerman, D. P. Walker, and Marilyn Williamson,[4] not to mention Mayerson herself, have disclosed the wealth of interpretations which the Orpheus legend had accumulated by the time it reached the Renaissance, while intensive scrutiny by such critics as Richard P. Adams, G. S. Fraser, Northrop Frye, and Rosemond Tuve[5] has yielded a wide variety of ingenious explanations of the role played in *Lycidas* by the Thracian singer. The lost metaphor has been comprehensively regained, or so it would seem. My chief contention in this chapter will be that in spite of all the attention it has received over the past twenty-five years or so, Milton's allusion to Orpheus has still not been fully understood.

Since the figure who has re-emerged from the underworld of medieval and Renaissance mythological commentary is somewhat complex, it might be useful before going any further to review the basic features of the original legend. Drawing mainly on Books X-XI of Ovid's *Metamorphoses* and Book IV of Virgil's *Georgics*, the two accounts which would have been most familiar to Milton's readers, Mayerson offers the following summary:

> Saddened by his second loss of Eurydice, Orpheus retreated from society in Rhodope, but he involuntarily attracted and enthralled with his music birds and beasts, even trees and stones. However, his followers were frightened away and Orpheus was killed and dismembered by the Bacchides. All nature mourned. The head and harp, thrown into the Hebrus, were carried to the sea and thence to Lesbos. There Apollo protected the head from a serpent's attack, and the Lesbians, having honored the remains by burial or by preservation in a temple, were rewarded with the gift of song.[6]

The question is: what does all this have to do with Edward King?

At the strictly literal level, it would be hard to improve on the answer first proposed by Thomas Warton, who observed with refreshing common sense that after the preceding reference to "the remorseless deep" (50) it was only natural to invoke the memory of Orpheus since he and Lycidas "were both victims of water."[7] Modern critics, on the other hand, have generally offered thematic rather than physical explanations for Orpheus' appearance in *Lycidas*. Rosemond Tuve, for example, asserts that Milton introduced him into the poem in order to show that "nothing is exempt [from death], not man's dearest hope or highest achievement; the principle of death in the universe has worsted what he thought confirmed his immorality, and nothing can outwit, nothing negate, that dark power. 'What could the Muse herself that Orpheus bore?'—not even the mother and source of that which allied him to the creating gods. All alike; down the swift Hebrus."[8] Richard P. Adams, Northrop Frye, and Caroline W. Mayerson draw rather less pessimistic inferences from the allusion, finding in it "a hint that Lycidas' recompense may parallel Orpheus',"[9] that he too will experience a form of "salvation out of water" analogous to the rebirth of Adonis at Byblos.[10] And G. S. Fraser, reviving (albeit unwittingly) a widespread medieval interpretation of Orpheus' descent into the underworld, suggests that "he is also a kind of prefiguration of Christ. Like Christ he descends into Hell and comes out again; but, where Christ harrows Hell, Orpheus

37

loses Eurydice at the last moment. Like Christ as the Logos, Orpheus harmonizes the natural world with his music. Like Christ he is cruelly sacrificed, but, unlike Christ, he has no resurrection."[11]

All three readings of the episode seem to me to be defective in one way or another. The first, as I shall show later, fails to take into account what is arguably the most essential factor linking Lycidas with Orpheus. The second and third are open to the rather more obvious objection that they are based upon precisely those elements in the original myth which Milton chose to leave out, namely Orpheus' attempt to rescue Eurydice from the realm of Pluto, and the fate of his head after it had reached "the Lesbian shore" (63). Fraser's christological interpretation, moreover, is vulnerable on yet another score: it does not differentiate between similarities and dissimilarities. Once the initial relationship between the two figures has been established, parallels and contrasts alike become grist to Fraser's analogizing mill. Thus the fact that Orpheus *resembled* Christ in descending into Hell is adduced as evidence in support of the same conclusion as the fact that Orpheus *differed* from Christ in returning from Hell empty-handed. With a critical method like that, virtually any character in the entire corpus of classical mythology could be transformed into a "kind of prefiguration of Christ."[12]

In any case, as I mentioned above, Milton did not treat Orpheus' journey into Hell, and in this he was typical of his age. For whereas medieval authors generally emphasized the quest for Eurydice with its obvious christological and moral overtones,[13] Renaissance poets and dramatists tended to focus their attention on the latter part of the story, which furnished them with a vivid illustration of the power of song to control both physical and psychological reality.[14] Although this theme was present in the myth from the very beginning, it was the humanists of the fifteenth and sixteenth centuries who, in Thomas H. Cain's words, brought Orpheus "to his fullest development as a prototype of the compellingly articulate man, the glorified orator or poet."[15] The deceptively simple lyric which opens Act III of Shakespeare's *Henry VIII* grows out of a rich interpretative tradition:

> Orpheus with his lute made trees
> And the mountain tops that freeze,
> Bow themselves when he did sing;
> To his music plants and flowers
> Ever sprung, as sun and showers
> There had made a lasting spring.

Everything that heard him play,
Even the billows of the sea,
Hung their heads and then lay by.
In sweet music is such art,
Killing care and grief of heart
Fall asleep and hearing die.[16]

Like the angelic choir in the *Nativity Ode*, the Muse's son can restore
the age of gold with his redemptive song.

If Milton's omission of Orpheus' adventures in the underworld was in
accord with current attitudes to the legend,[17] however, his emphasis on
the Bacchantes' assault and the Muse's impotence was highly unortho-
dox. The author of *Lycidas*, Mayerson remarks in passing, "appears to
be unique among his contemporaries and predecessors in making a poetic
adaptation of the death of Orpheus."[18] The point is more important, I
think, than she herself seems to have recognized. For by focusing upon
the one episode in Orpheus' career which suggested that in the final
analysis poetry was powerless to affect history, Milton was not only
expressing his poetic originality; he was giving the lie to one of the most
revered beliefs in European literary culture.

He was also rejecting his own interpretation of the story in such earlier
works as *L'Allegro*, *Il Penseroso*, and *Ad Patrem*, where the Thracian
singer appears in his conventional Renaissance guise as "a symbol of
poetry's power to control and civilize."[19] The allusion to him in the last
of these poems is particularly interesting in connection with *Lycidas*, for
whether we agree with Grierson and Tillyard that it was composed not
long before 1637 or with the editors of the *Variorum Commentary* that
it was written in 1631,[20] the Latin epistle is clearly related to the English
elegy in a number of ways. The parallel between the "inenarrabile carmen" which Milton mentions to his father and the "unexpressive nuptial
Song" (176) overheard by Edward King has often been noticed,[21] but
there are many other similarities between the two works in both phraseology and conception. The opening description of the Muse "meditating"
(7) her song in *Ad Patrem* anticipates the poet's obligation to "meditate" (66) the Muse in *Lycidas*; "aurea Clio" (14) has her counterpart
in the "golden hayrd Calliope" of Milton's original draft for the later
poem; the account of Olympus adumbrates most of the features which
characterize "the blest Kingdoms meek of joy and love" (177); the ivy
and laurel of the victor's crown reappear as the symbols of Bacchus and
Apollo; and the youthful poet who is no longer content to remain

"obscurus" (103) survives as the "uncouth Swain" (186) mourning for Lycidas.

By far the most important connection between the two works, however, is their common concern with the nature and worth of the poetic vocation. As critics of the earlier poem are fond of saying, *Ad Patrem* is Milton's *Defence of Poetry*. In view of the general line of defence he pursues, it might equally well be called his *Canonization*. For just as Donne refuses to "observe his honour, or his grace, Or the king's reall, or his stamped face" (6-7), so Milton rejects "the golden hope of storing away money" and "the laws, the ill-guarded statutes of our nation" (70-72); just as Donne retires to the "hermitage" of perfectly fulfilled sexuality, so Milton takes refuge from "the uproar of the city" in "seclusions deep . . . amid the delightful leisure of the Aonian stream" where he can walk "a blessed comrade at Apollo's side" (74-76). The only difference is that the Puritan poet determines to abandon the world of commerce and politics for the sake not of love but of literature. In the Arcadian security of his studies at Horton, he asserts, he will be invulnerable to the ills which afflict those who have chosen to pursue wealth or public office:

Keep yourselves far away, wakeful Cares, keep yourselves far away, Complaints, and the eye of Envy with its crooked lear. Stretch not wide, merciless Calumny, your snake-bearing jaws. Most loathsome crew, you possess naught of baneful power against me, nor am I in your control. Safe, with breast secure, I shall stride on, uplifted high from your viper blows. (105-10)

This boundless confidence in the Muse's capacity to protect her followers from the hostility of a corrupt society is matched only by Milton's faith in her followers' capacity to persuade that society to act less corruptly. There is virtually nothing, he assures his father, that human eloquence cannot accomplish when it is divinely inspired. Poets are the acknowledged legislators of the world, and their original prototype is Orpheus, "who by his songs . . . held fast the streams, and added ears to the oaks by his songs . . . and by his singing compelled to tears the shades that were done with life" (52-55).

It is a far cry from this majestic figure to the helpless victim of "the rout that made the hideous roar" (61). Even though they both derive from the original myth, the Orpheus whose song could make rivers stand still in *Ad Patrem* and the Orpheus whose "goary visage down the stream was sent" (62) in *Lycidas* are scarcely recognizable as the same character. The one seems to belong to the sunlit lanscapes of Theocritus' seventh *Idyl*; the other to the joyless and decaying world of Virgil's ninth *Eclogue*.[22] Milton could hardly have given us a more precise or vivid way of measuring the impact which the death of Edward King must have had upon his conception of the poetic vocation. The youthful optimism which had animated the epistle to his father has collapsed in a nightmare of senseless destruction which even the Muse was powerless to prevent. Critics like Adams and Fraser who insist on superimposing upon that vision the less gloomy aspects of the Orpheus legend do violence not only to the text of *Lycidas* but to the intensity of Milton's desperation at this juncture of the poem. Of the three readings of the episode I summarized earlier only Tuve's recognizes the profound pessimism which informs Milton's allusion to the Muse's "inchanting son" (59).

What Tuve's interpretation does not recognize is the fundamental source of Milton's pessimism, which has to do not so much with the fact of Orpheus' death as with the circumstances surrounding it. Ovid describes them as follows:

Throughout this time [that is, after his failure to rescue Eurydice] Orpheus had shrunk from loving any woman, either because of his unhappy experience, or because he had pledged himself not to do so. In spite of this there were many who were fired with a desire to marry the poet, many who were indignant to find themselves repulsed. However, Orpheus preferred to centre his affections on boys of tender years, and to enjoy the brief spring and early flowering of their youth; he was the first to introduce this custom among the people of Thrace.... Looking down from the crest of a hill, the female followers of Bacchus, with animal skins slung across their breasts, saw Orpheus as he was singing and accompanying himself on the lyre. One of them, tossing her hair till it streamed in the light breeze, cried out: "See! Look here! Here is the man who scorns us!" and flung her spear at the poet Apollo loved, at the lips which produced such melodies.... All their weapons would have been rendered harmless by the charm of Orpheus' songs, but clamorous shouting, Phrygian flutes with curving horns, tambourines, the beating of breasts, and Bacchic howlings, drowned the music of the lyre. Then at last the stones grew crimson with the blood of the poet, whose voice they did not hear.... Hurling their leaf-decked thyrsi, made for a far different purpose, the women launched their attack on the poet.... Dead to all reverence, they tore him apart and, through those lips to which rocks had listened, which wild beasts had understood, his last breath slipped away and vanished in the wind.[23]

Critics of *Lycidas* have persistently refused to acknowledge that the mainspring of this part of the Orpheus legend is the theme of sexual (or rather of heterosexual) abstinence. Mayerson's summary, which I quoted above, bowdlerizes the most crucial element in the story—"retreated from Society"[24] hardly does justice to Ovid's explicit description of Orpheus' misogyny—and the explanation in the *Variorum Commentary* is equally mealy-mouthed. "After his final loss of Eurydice," we are told, "Orpheus roamed his native Thrace, lamenting his loss and charming with his song all nature, animate and inanimate. Enraged by his devotion to his dead wife and his implied scorn of them, the frenzied Maenads attacked him."[25]

Medieval commentators, though clearly embarrassed by the pederastic inclinations of one of their favourite Christ-figures, were at least willing to confront Ovid's text in its entirety. Taking their cue from Boethius, who had interpreted Orpheus' love for Eurydice as an example of reason's submission to passion,[26] they allegorized his subsequent distaste for women as a victory over carnal concupiscence. On account of the loss of Eurydice, wrote Giovanni del Virgilio:

> Orpheus renounced Hell, that is, temptation, and reconciling himself to God began to spurn women, giving his soul instead to God, and began to love men, that is, to act in a manly way, on which account he was dead to the delights of the world; for such men are dead to the world.[27]

And Arnulf of Orleans explained that Orpheus "shunned women, that is, those acting in a womanlike manner, drunkards and vicious men, but transferred his love to men, that is, to those acting in a manly way."[28]

By the seventeenth century this moralistic reading of the episode had coalesced with Boccaccio's humanistic interpretation of the conclusion of the story according to which the snake stood for "the circling years . . . which tried to devour Orpheus' head—that is, his name or rather those works Orpheus composed by his genius . . . while the powers of imagination throve in his head. The snake is said to be turned into stone, however, to show that time can in no way put Orpheus down."[29] The result was the characteristically Renaissance version of the legend to be found in Bacon's *Wisdom of the Ancients* and Sandys' commentary on the *Metamorphoses*. Orpheus was averse from women, they both argue, because "the sweets of marriage and the dearness of children commonly draw men away from performing great and lofty services to the commonwealth; being content to be perpetuated in their race and stock, and not in their deeds."[30]

For most of Milton's readers, then, the Muse's son was not simply a poet. He was a poet who, in Sandys' words, judged "the propagation of wisdome and virtuous endeavours" by means of poetry to be "more noble and immortall than that of posterity."[31] Which is precisely how Milton himself had described Orpheus in the *Elegia Sexta* just eight years before the composition of *Lycidas*:

> But if a poet sings of wars, of Heaven controlled by a Jove full grown, of duty-doing heroes, of captains that are half gods, if he sings now the holy counsels of the gods above, now the realms below wherein howls a savage hound, let him live a simple frugal life, after the fashion of the teacher who came from Samos, let herbs offer him food that works no harm, let pellucid water stand near him, in a tiny cup of beechen wood, and let him drink only sober draughts from a pure spring. On such a poet are imposed, too, a youth free of crime, pure and chaste, and a character unyielding, and a name without taint; such an one must he be as you are, augur, as, resplendent with holy vestments and with lustral waters, you rise, minded to go forth to face the angry gods. In this way, story says, wise Tiresias lived, after the light had been swept away from him, and Ogygian Linus, and Calchas, exiled from his hearth, ... and aged Orpheus, in the lonely grots, after he had tamed the wild beasts. (55-70)

In Milton's eyes, as in his contemporaries', Orpheus was an exemplar not only of poetic eloquence but of the abstemiousness necessary to achieve it. In the Renaissance the source of inspiration was to be found in the tub of Diogenes rather than the wound of Philoctetes.

It was this aspect of the myth which I had in mind when I claimed earlier that Tuve's commentary fails to take account of the most crucial factor linking Orpheus with Edward King. For what the Greek poet and his seventeenth-century successor have in common is their refusal to sport with Amaryllis in the shade, and what makes their deaths so profoundly disquieting to Milton is the inability of their innocence to keep the blind fury at bay. Although his devotion to chastity was no doubt as sincere as the Lady's in *Comus*, no "glistring Guardian" descended to keep King's life "unassail'd" (218-19), while Orpheus' newly won abstinence, far from dashing "brute violence" (450), apparently provoked it. The son of Calliope was "torne in peeces by women," explained Thomas Cooper in his *Dictionarium Historicum et Poeticum*, "because that for the sorow of his wyfe Eurydice he did not onely himselfe refuse the love of many women, and lyved a sole lyfe, but also disswaded others from the company of women."[32] Coming immediately after the address to the nymphs with its implicit suggestion that by renouncing the pleas-

43

ures of the flesh you may be able to escape the fate of a Daphnis or a Gallus, Milton's reference to Orpheus' death thus serves as a devastating counter-example.[33] For as we have seen, the point of the *ubi eratis* topos in the sixteenth and seventeenth centuries was not so much the saving power of the Muses as the saving power of chastity and retirement. If only the protagonists of the first *Idyl* and the tenth *Eclogue* had not succumbed to "unbeseeming love"[34] they might have survived to write more poetry, or so the commentators believed. The gruesome scene on the banks of the Hebrus totally subverts this simple-minded faith in the efficacy of pastoral virtue. Despite their determination to scorn delights and live laborious days, both Orpheus and his seventeenth-century counterpart had gone "down the stream"[35] with Daphnis anyway.

Tuve is only partly right, therefore, when she states that the function of the allusion is to remind us "that deathless poetry is not deathless, that nothing is."[36] To the author of the *Elegia Sexta, Ad Patrem,* and *Comus,* the most appalling thing about the death of Orpheus must surely have been its injustice rather than its inevitability. The self-denial which Milton had always assumed to be a prerequisite for writing great poetry could evidently have the very same consequences as the sensual indulgence which brought Daphnis and Gallus to their untimely ends. Atropos did not distinguish between bucolic innocence and courtly vice. "Et in Arcadia ego."

CHAPTER SIX

The Thankless Muse

The bitter questions which follow the Orpheus episode have often been called digressive, as though they had little or nothing to do with the rest of the poem. Even a critic as sensitive to structural relationships as Roy Daniells hints that there may be a disjunction at this point of the elegy. "The window onto this vision of ghastly dismemberment instantly shuts," he writes. "A meditation on Fame ensues. This is all the more strange because we know from other evidence how fully the Orpheus myth had established itself in Milton's consciousness."[1] Were there no connection at all between the vision and the meditation, as Daniells' account suggests, the lack of continuity certainly would be strange. But once the real nature of the Orpheus allusion has been recognized, it should be readily apparent that Milton's misgivings about the worth of the homely slighted shepherd's trade are anything but a sudden or unexpected interruption. On the contrary, they are the logical culmination of a train of thought that began with the address to the nymphs. If in fact it makes no difference whether one obeys or disobeys the rules traditionally associated with the figures of Daphnis and Gallus, and exemplified by the latter part of Orpheus' career, then the questions Milton asks are not merely relevant. They are inescapable:

> Alas! What boots it with uncessant care
> To tend the homely slighted Shepherds trade,
> And strictly meditate the thankless Muse?
> Were it not better don as others use,
> To sport with Amaryllis in the shade,
> Or with the tangles of Neaera's hair? (64-69)

The sense of release in these lines is almost as powerful as the sense of angry bafflement they simultaneously express. Like Arethusa's stream, the undercurrent of anxiety which has slowly been gathering strength beneath the allusions to Daphnis, Gallus, and Orpheus has finally broken through to the surface.[2]

That it should prove to be such intensely sexual anxiety should come as no surprise after all the doubts that those allusions have tacitly directed at the ideal of chastity. Once again "the sage And serious doctrine of Virginity" (787) is under attack, but its assailant is no longer a mere belly-god with his cup of cordial julep but the blind Fury with her shears, and what is at stake on this occasion is not the honour of an earl's daughter but the future career of an epic poet. For Milton's sustained outburst of self-interrogation challenges the fundamental principle upon which his whole conception of the poetic vocation had been based: the denial of the flesh. In a youthful sonnet to the nightingale he had assured the bird that "Whether the Muse, or Love call thee his mate, Both them I serve, and of their train am I" (13-14). Long before he wrote *Lycidas*, however, he had come to believe that such a divided loyalty was impossible and had abandoned Love in order to serve the Muse more faithfully. Now that she has proved to be as "thankless" (66)[3] as the "cruelfair" of the courtly tradition, he could hardly avoid wondering whether he had made the right choice when he renounced love. Perhaps, after all, the suppression of the erotic impulse was too high a price to pay for an art he might never survive to practise. At last the issue originally adumbrated by the juxtaposition of the laurel and the myrtle in the opening lines of the poem is out in the open. What possible justification can there be for worshipping Apollo to the exclusion of Venus when the reward for your fidelity is withdrawn just as you are preparing to receive it? Wouldn't it be more sensible to follow Volpone's advice and prove "while we may, the sports of love"?[4] Better, surely, to risk gathering the rosebuds too soon than to suffer the fate of the "rathe primrose" which, in an earlier draft of the poem, died "unwedded," "colouring the pale cheek of uninjoyed love."[5]

To assume with several recent critics that Amaryllis and Neaera stand for no more than the composition of love poetry as opposed to epic poetry is, therefore, to misunderstand the whole tenor of Milton's argument. The alternative which has gradually emerged during the previous thirteen lines is not the writing of a different kind of poem; it is the living of a different kind of life. Whatever symbolic overtones the two nymphs may have acquired as a result of their association with the amatory verse of George Buchanan, the most important thing about them, as E. S. LeComte rightly reminds us,[6] is that they are girls.

In particular, we may note in passing, they are the girls whose presence distracts the shepherds from their pastoral labours in Virgil's Arcadia. Amaryllis makes her first appearance at the beginning of *Eclogue I* as Meliboeus is contrasting Tityrus' good fortune with his own unhappy plight:

You Tityrus, lie under your spreading beech's covert, wooing the woodland Muse on slender reed, but we are leaving our country's bounds and sweet fields. We are outcasts from our country; you Tityrus, at ease beneath the shade, teach the woods to echo 'fair Amaryllis'. (1-5)

She reappears in *Eclogue II* as Corydon recalls how he courted her before he fell in love with the cruel Alexis. "Was it not better," he asks himself, "to brook Amaryllis' sullen rage and scornful disdain?" (14-15). Milton's allusion to her characteristically fuses the two passages into a single reference[7]—his "meditate the thankless Muse" is clearly a variant of Virgil's "silvestrem . . . musam meditaris" while "in the shade" and "Were it not better done" translate the Latin phrases "in umbra" and "nonne fuit satius" word for word. Read in this dual context, the notion of sporting with Amaryllis reverberates with ironies. Milton is proposing to abandon a thankless mistress for a nymph who was as well known for her disdain as for her beauty, and he is proposing to do so at precisely that moment in history when another group of shepherds is being deprived of its pastoral living by the tyranny of an unjust administration. Confronted by the possibility that his "laborious days" have all been wasted, Meliboeus is offering to change places with Tityrus.

This latter theme is reinforced by the association which the name of Neaera would have been likely to stir in the minds of Milton's readers. In Virgil's *Eclogue III* it is Neaera who is responsible for Aegon's refusal to take proper care of his flock:

Poor sheep, ever luckless flock, While your master courts Neaera and fears lest she prefer Menalcas to him, this hireling keeper milks his ewes twice an hour, and the flock are robbed of strength and the lambs of milk. (3-6)

Long before St. Peter appears on the scene to foretell "the ruine of our corrupted Clergie," his complaints about faithless herdsmen have been anticipated by the elegist's Virgilian allusions.[8] In the very act of naming the representatives of erotic pleasure in *Lycidas*, Milton has provided himself (and us) with at least a potential reason for rejecting them.

For the time being, though, a motive so closely related to the ecclesiastical aspect of the pastoral metaphor can be no more than potential. Not until the arrival of the "Pilot of the Galilean lake" (109) will Edward King assume his role as a potential churchman. Here he is still a poet, and the immediate issue, as I have emphasized, is not the integrity of Christ's ministers but the chastity of the Muse's followers. Milton's treatment of this issue in the lines which follow owes a great deal of its power, I suspect, to the intimate connection that existed in his own mind between poetic productivity on the one hand and sexual abstinence on the other. For when the pursuit of any activity is made dependent upon the avoidance of some other, the first often turns out to be a sublimated version of the second. Alternatives, in other words, have a way of becoming substitutes. So by insisting that the poetic impulse could not be fulfilled unless the erotic impulse was repressed, Milton was in effect creating an equivalence between them. Apollo takes the place of Venus, Calliope assumes the role of Amaryllis, and her devotees make poems instead of love.

It was only natural, then, that Milton should have equated the frustration of literary potentiality with the denial of sexual fulfilment. Given the correspondence worked out by Sandys and Bacon between the two kinds of propagation,[9] to cut off the possibility of great literary works was analogous to destroying the opportunity to beget children. As a result, the assault of the abhorred shears feels like a castration:

> Fame is the spur that the clear spirit doth raise
> (That last infirmity of Noble mind)
> To scorn delights, and live laborious dayes;
> But the fair Guerdon when we hope to find,
> And think to burst out into sudden blaze,
> Comes the blind Fury with th' abhorred shears,
> And slits the thin spun life. (70-76)

Beneath Milton's decorous periphrases one can sense in these lines an urgency and excitement which seem to me to be essentially sexual in nature. The tumescent implications of raising "the clear spirit" are obvious, especially when we remember that in the seventeenth century the word "spirit" could mean, among other things, semen.[10] The "fair Guerdon" to which it aspires could well be a courtly euphemism for the usual reward bestowed by merciful ladies upon their faithful lovers. And it would be hard to improve upon the phrase "burst out into sudden blaze" as a description of an orgasm. The barely submerged sexuality of Milton's language thus turns the pursuit of fame into an act of love. But the anticipated climax never takes place. The blind fury comes instead.[11]

Phoebus Apollo's response to this crisis is generally agreed to be inadequate, either because it is couched in pagan rather than in Christian terms, or because it sounds too pat and aphoristic.[12] The foregoing analysis suggests another and more serious reason for the failure of his admonitions to convince: they completely miss the point, which had to do not so much with losing fame as with losing the chance to earn it. By touching Milton's ear, as he had touched Virgil's in the sixth *Eclogue*,[13] Phoebus seems to imply that the Puritan poet is getting above himself. But in fact the issue here is not pride, or praise, or even fame. It is fulfilment. Confronted with the possibility that he may never be allowed to run the race for which he has spent most of his adult life training himself, what possible consolation can Milton be expected to find in the announcement that the prize-giving will be in heaven? Divine approval of the rigour of his preparations would no doubt be gratifying, but it would hardly compensate for the utter futility of undertaking them. The solution simply does not address the problem, and one is left with a sense of incompleteness, of answers yet to be given.[14]

Yet however unsuccessful the arguments themselves may be, it is particularly appropriate that the voice which expounds them should be Phoebus Apollo's. For in addition to being the god of poetry, Phoebus was also the husband of the Muse whom Milton was threatening to desert and, still more significantly, the father of the poet whose death at the hands of the Bacchantes had prompted those thoughts of desertion. Orpheus, declared Thomas Cooper, was "the son (as some write) of Apollo and Calliope,"[15] and despite his cautious parenthesis virtually every Renaissance scholar who considered the question held the same opinion. The advice Milton receives, therefore, comes from someone who has suffered a loss quite as grievous as his own, and as a result it has a special kind of authenticity. As god of poetry alone, Phoebus might have been suspected of defending his own interests when he attempts to provide the poet with a reason for continuing to serve the Muse. As the bereaved father of Orpheus, on the other hand, he has more reason to share Milton's outraged feelings than to soothe them. Far from being the impersonal observations of an insensitive *deus ex machina*, Phoebus' speech implicitly exemplifies the patience it advocates.

CHAPTER SEVEN

The Hungry Sheep

In a transformation that is typical of the poem as a whole, what at one moment appeared to be a provisional kind of ending at the next moment proves to have been the beginning of a completely new phase in the poem's development. For when we first came to Phoebus' discourse on fame, it sounded no less conclusive than the revelations of Patience in *Sonnet XIX*.[1] As soon as Camus and the Pilot of the Galilean Lake arrive on the scene, however, we realize that the god of poetry not only brought the opening movement of the elegy to a close; he simultaneously initiated the second movement, the procession of visitors. This radical readjustment in our perception of Phoebus' role may already have been suggested, of course, by a detail which to Milton's classically trained readers would have seemed only too obvious: Phoebus is the first of the three divinities who come to visit the dying Gallus in Virgil's tenth *Eclogue*. In which case it may not be too fanciful to hear in the god's admonitions in *Lycidas* a faint echo of his outburst in the *Eclogue*: "Gallus, what madness this? Thy sweetheart Lycoris hath followed another amid snows and amid rugged camps" (22-23).[2] Both the classical and the puritan poets have been seeking fulfilment in the wrong place.

Certainly there is a close relationship between the second visitors in the two elegies. Virgil's Silvanus, who came "with rustic glories on his brow, waving his fennel flowers and tall lilies" (24-26) is clearly the prototype of Milton's Camus with his "Mantle hairy, and his Bonnet sedge, Inwrought with figures dim, and on the edge Like to that sanguine flower inscrib'd with woe" (104-06).[3] The one significant characteristic that distinguishes Camus from his Virgilian predecessor is his fatherhood. While it is true, as several scholars have remarked, that rivers are often paternal (Old Father Thames and *Pater Tiber* for example), I suspect that Milton may have had another reason for introducing a parent at this juncture of the poem: in Theocritus' first *Idyl* the visitors are headed by Hermes, Daphnis' father. Given the link which I suggested earlier between *Lycidas* and *Ad Patrem*,[4] the relationship between Hermes and Daphnis in the *Idyl* might have been the only stimulus Milton needed to portray King's first formal mourner as a

father too. After Milton had so confidently proclaimed the poet's in-
vulnerability in a poem addressed to his own father, it seems only natural
that it should be Lycidas' "reverend Sire" (103)[5] who returns to mourn
the forfeiture of his "dearest pledge" (107).[6]

The relationship between the third visitor and the corresponding
characters in the first *Idyl* and the tenth *Eclogue* is still more complex.
In the first *Idyl* the Pilot's counterpart is Venus, who comes to gloat over
the downfall of her mortal antagonist:

> Now came also sweet Cypris with laughter in her heart but making a
> show of heavy wrath, and she said "Surely, thou didst boast, Daphnis,
> that thou wouldst throw Love for a fall; but hast thou not rather thyself
> been thrown by irresistible Love?" (95-98)

After the foregoing analysis of the address to the nymphs and the allusion
to Orpheus, the implications of Milton's decision to substitute St. Peter[7]
for Venus hardly require comment. It is worth noting, nevertheless, how
completely the Christian saint reverses the image of the pagan goddess.
His wrath, for instance, is genuine, not affected, and its object is no
longer the abstemiousness of a real shepherd but the self-indulgence of
false ones:

> How well could I have spar'd for thee, young swain,
> Anow of such as for their bellies sake,
> Creep and intrude, and climb into the fold?
> Of other care they little reck'ning make,
> Then how to scramble at the shearers feast,
> And shove away the worthy bidden guest;
> Blind mouthes! (113-19)

The only common element is the grim satisfaction with which both
speakers contemplate the irony of their enemies' punishments: just as
Daphnis, the would-be overthrower, has himself been overthrown, so, St.
Peter promises, the faithless sheep-shearers are eventually destined to be
shorn by "that two-handed engine at the door" (130).[8] Divine justice is
no less "irresistible" than human love.

In the *Eclogue* the last visitor is Pan, the god of shepherds, who was
to become one of the standard types of Christ in the mythological trea-
tises of the Middle Ages and the Renaissance.[9] Virgil describes his arrival
as follows:

> Pan came, Arcady's god and we ourselves saw him, crimsoned with ver-
> milion and blood-red elderberries. "Will there be no end?" he cried.

51

"Love recks naught of this: neither is cruel Love sated with tears, nor the grass with the rills, nor bees with the clover, nor goats with leaves." (26-30) [10]

Here, perhaps, is the source of the digestive metaphor in St. Peter's speech—Riccius' *Paraphrasis* even substitutes sheep (*oves*) for Virgil's bees (*apes*). [11] But once again the basic pattern of the original passage has been transposed. St. Peter's point is not that the sheep are insatiable but that the shepherds are unwilling to satisfy them. What in the *Eclogue* was an illustration of the futility of grief has become in *Lycidas* a reason for succumbing to it.

The most important difference between the Pilot of the Galilean lake and his two classical predecessors, however, concerns the audience rather than the content of his speech. In both the *Idyl* and the *Eclogue* the visitors came to persuade the protagonist to abandon a way of life which was likely to prove fatal. In *Lycidas* the protagonist is already dead, and the visitors come not to admonish but to mourn him. It is too late for Edward King to change his mind. But it is not too late for Milton. Unlike Lycidas, the lonely shepherd who has survived to weep this "melodious tear" (14) still has time to ponder the revelations delivered by Phoebus and St. Peter. Indeed, the speech of the first visitor, as we now recognize him to have been, was specifically addressed to King's elegist. For a few moments, at least, the singer was in the position traditionally occupied by the hero of his song, [12] and although the third visitor ostensibly directs his comments to the dead "young swain" (113) beneath the Irish Sea it is the "uncouth Swain" (186) still living among the oaks and rills who actually hears them.

I do not think he can have found them very consoling. If, as I argued earlier, Phoebus Apollo's attempts to comfort the "homely slighted Shepherd" (65) rang somewhat hollow, St. Peter's enigmatic promise to avenge the "hungry Sheep" (125) sounds almost irrelevant. For one thing, after the vehemence of the complaint, the couplet containing the remedy seems altogether too pat. [13] For another, the remedy itself will not take effect until the day of judgement. To a sensibility as passionately concerned as Milton's certainly was with the social and political realities of his immediate situation, an eschatological punishment for present crimes must have been no more satisfying than an eschatological compensation for present injuries. In G. S. Fraser's words, Milton was not "by temperament the kind of man who would wait patiently for the Day of Judgement for his enemies to get their deserts." [14] The most important question for him was always: what should be done *now*? Granted that

St. Michael's sword[15] will smite the faithless herdsmen on the last day, how is the flock to be protected in the meantime? Can ecclesiastical reform be left in abeyance merely because self-seeking ministers are destined to be punished "at the door" (130)? Shouldn't some attempt be made to remedy the current condition of the church, to banish false shepherds from the fold and hunt down the wolf in his lair?

That Milton was troubled by such questions appears all the more likely when we follow the advice of several recent commentators and compare St. Peter's condemnation of "our corrupted Clergie" in *Lycidas* with his fiery imprecations against the papacy in *The Divine Comedy*:

> I flash and redden, seeing these things done.
> From here above, preying on every fold
> In shepherds' clothing wolves are seen to slink:
> O succour of God, thy hand why doest thou hold?
> . . .
>
> But the high Providence, which with Scipio's might
> Rescued the glory of the world for Rome,
> Soon will bring help, if I conceive aright.[16]

A millennial solution to a contemporary problem would never satisfy Dante's St. Peter. Providence, he maintains, cannot remain aloof for very much longer; unless it acts "soon" the wolves will devour the entire flock. If C. H. Herford, K. McKenzie and others are correct in thinking that Milton had these lines in mind while he was composing his own denunciation of ecclesiastical corruption,[17] it is difficult to believe that he could have been unmoved by the sense of urgency which they convey.

The plight of the sheep in *Lycidas* is thrown into still sharper relief by one of Milton's most significant (though least noted) departures from the pastoral tradition: his violation of the long-standing convention whereby the sheep are delegated to the care of a companion while the shepherd himself is performing the song. During the opening exchanges of Theocritus' first *Idyl*, for instance, Thyrsis accompanies his invitation to "sit down here, goatherd, on this hill slope by the tamarisks and play your pipe" with an offer to "tend your goats meanwhile" (12-14). And although Mopsus needs no persuasion to lament the death of Daphnis in Virgil's fifth *Eclogue*, Menalcas nevertheless assures him that while he is singing "Tityrus will tend the grazing kids" (12). For the duration of *Lycidas*, on the contrary, no one is tending the flock. Milton is warbling his Doric lay, and Edward King is dead. In the meantime, as the references to Amaryllis and Neaera have already hinted,[18] the sheepfold has been left to the mercies of ignorant and greedy hirelings. Like the lambs in the *Epitaphium Damonis* who "go home unpastured" because their "master" is too busy singing his song to attend to them (18), the "hungry Sheep" are starving for want of adequate nourishment. The absence of the shepherd's traditional companion from Milton's elegy thus poses an obvious question. Instead of playing on his "Oaten Flute" (33) shouldn't the uncouth swain be feeding the flock himself? Were it not better done, if not to sport with Amaryllis in the shade, at least to labour for St. Peter in the sheepfold? Instead of writing poems, shouldn't John Milton be ministering to the religious needs of his fellow countrymen?[19]

For a long time, of course, that is exactly what he had planned to do. According to the autobiographical preface to Book II of *Reason of Church Government*, Milton was destined for the ministry both "by the intentions of my parents and friends" and "in mine own resolutions." But, as he goes on to explain, "perceaving what tyranny had invaded the Church" he had subsequently abandoned his plans to enter holy orders, and he had decided to devote himself wholly to poetry. Unfortunately, Milton does not tell us when precisely this decision was taken, merely that he was "Church-outed by the Prelats" when he had arrived at "some maturity of years."[20] We cannot, therefore, be certain whether or not he still hoped to pursue an ecclesiastical career when he wrote *Lycidas*. If John Spencer Hill is right in believing that Milton did not abandon his plans for a career in the church until the promulgation of the *Constitutions and Canons Ecclesiastical* in 1640,[21] then the plight of the neglected flock must surely have exacerbated the anxiety he felt about his delay in entering the priesthood. For ever since he became eligible for ordination on his twenty-fourth birthday in 1632 he had been open to the charge of procrastination. The carefully composed letter to an unidentified friend in 1633 reveals that Milton, after only a year's delay, felt obliged to defend his "tardie moving." He has not, he insists, given himself up "to dreame away my yeares in the arms of studious retirement like Endymion with the Moone."[22] "Something suspicious" of his own nature, he is well aware of "a certaine belatednesse" in his progress towards the pulpit, but he asks his friend to believe that it is due to his wish "to be more fit" rather than to any "endlesse delight of speculation." If this is any indication of Milton's mood in 1633 when Laud had just been elevated to the archbishopric of Canterbury, how must he have felt four years later when the effects of Laud's policies were only too evident?

Assuming, on the other hand, that Milton had abandoned his intention to enter the priesthood before he composed *Lycidas*, the situation he describes in St. Peter's speech must surely have given him some qualms about his decision to devote himself entirely to poetry. It is true, of course, that in the *Elegia Sexta* and elsewhere he describes the poetic vocation as a kind of priesthood, declaring that the poet's character, should be like the seer's "as, resplendent with holy vestments and with lustral waters, you rise, minded to go forth to face the angry gods. . . . For the bard is sacred to the gods, he is priest of the gods" (65-77). Like the biblical prophet, he believed, the poet was "toucht with hallow'd fire," capable of restoring the golden age by the transforming power of his song.[23] But here in *Lycidas* the death of Edward King has brought him face to face with the possibility that he had been over-estimating the power of poetry. Suppose, after all, that the poet's voice was not capable of replacing the preacher's? Suppose, in W. H. Auden's words, that "poetry makes nothing happen," surviving merely "in the valley of its saying"?[24] If Orpheus' song could not allay the perturbations of the Bacchantes, what hope could Milton have of charming their seventeenth-century counterparts? Won't the lean and flashy songs of false shepherds drown out his music just as surely as the hideous roar of the Maenads overwhelmed the song of Orpheus? Perhaps Milton's mouth, too, is blind. The headnote added to the 1645 edition of *Lycidas* may affirm the prophetic efficacy of Milton's words, but in 1637 when the corrupted clergy was "in their height," there was no reason to suppose that the Laudian church was destined to collapse so soon. St. Peter's speech thus serves to intensify, not assuage, the anxieties which we saw earlier were implicit in the poem's title. Far from being a digression, as it is still sometimes called,[25] it touches on the central issue of Milton's entire career. In a land threatened by wolves, who will listen to the shepherd's piping?

The predicament of the hungry sheep thus drives a wedge between the two major referents of the pastoral metaphor. The life of the shepherd-poet is implicitly presented as an alternative to that of the shepherd-priest, an alternative which in the historical circumstances of 1637 may not have had very much to recommend it. "At the centre of pastoral," Paul Alpers has written in an illuminating essay, "is the shepherd-singer. The great pastoral poets are directly concerned with the extent to which song that gives present pleasures can confront and, if not transform and celebrate, then accept and reconcile man to the stresses and realities of his situation."[26] In *Lycidas*, the extent to which song can accomplish these ends is problematical. Far from recording Milton's discovery of his role as a divinely inspired epic poet, as Donald Friedman has argued in a recent article,[27] Milton's elegy calls into question the efficacy of the poetic vocation itself. The traditional pastoral *topos* of the reward for good singing has acquired a new dimension.

In a last despairing attempt, perhaps, to test the power of song, Milton invokes the Sicilian muse of Theocritus (rather than the more pessimistic Virgil) to sing one of the most elaborately and self-consciously poetic passages in the entire poem. Like so much else in *Lycidas* it gains significance if it is read against the background of the first *Idyl* and the tenth *Eclogue*. In both works, immediately after the speech of the final visitor the dying lover summons up his strength to deliver one final speech. After taunting Cypris for loving Adonis, Daphnis bids farewell to the pastoral world and prophesies the changes in the natural order which will follow his death:

> Now you may bear violets, you bramble bushes; bear them, you thistles, and let the lovely narcissus spread its foliage over the juniper. Let all things be changed, and let the pine tree bear pears, since Daphnis dies, and let the stag drag down the dogs and let the screech owl from the mountains contend with the nightingales. (132-36)

Gallus, on the contrary, imagines an ideal landscape in which he might have disported himself if only he had been an Arcadian shepherd:

> And O that I had been one of you, the shepherd of a flock of yours, or the dresser of your ripened grapes! Surely, my darling, whether it were Phyllis or Amyntas, or whoever it were—and what if Amyntas be dark? violets, too, are black and black are hyacinths—my darling would be lying at my side among the willows under the creeping vine—Phyllis culling me garlands, Amyntas singing songs. Here are cool springs, Lycoris, here soft meadows, here woodland; here, with thee, time alone would wear me away. (35-43)[28]

In *Lycidas*, however, the protagonist is already dead, so in place of Edward King's voice we hear his elegist's:[29]

> And call the Vales, and bid them hither cast
> Their Bells, and Flourets of a thousand hues.
> Ye valleys low where the milde whispers use,
> Of shades and wanton winds and gushing brooks,
> On whose fresh lap the swart Star sparely looks,
> Throw hither all your quaint enameld eyes,
> That on the green terf suck the honied showres,
> And purple all the ground with vernal flowres.
> . . .
> To strew the Laureat Herse where Lycid lies. (134-51)

,The vision is still essentially pastoral but now it is unpopulated by any living human presence. Whereas Gallus imagines himself lying in a pastoral bower beside his mistress, Lycidas lies on a laureate hearse alone. Or so Milton imagines for a moment. In fact, as he recognizes immediately afterwards, the actual situation is still further removed from that in the *Eclogue*. Virgil's cool springs have given way to the "sounding Seas" (154), and King's body is lost beneath the "whelming tide" (157).[30] As a result, the attempt to interpose some pastoral "ease" (152) collapses in the face of reality; decking a drowned man with flowers, Milton realizes, is like feeding the sheep with wind. So the preceding fiction and all it stands for is dismissed as a "false surmise" (153). Poetry has attempted to perform its consolatory office, and it has failed.

CHAPTER EIGHT

Joy and Love

Of all the reversals we have so far encountered in *Lycidas*, Milton's emphatic command to "Weep no more" (165) is easily the most violent. Without any apparent reason, the whole poem suddenly changes direction. Pagan myths give way to Christian revelation, despair turns into ecstasy, and the nightmare of a monstrous world beneath the waves is displaced by a vision of "the blest Kingdoms meek" (177) above the sky. Yet despite its abruptness, the assertion that Edward King is still alive does not take us entirely by surprise. There are several reasons for this. First, the apotheosis of the dead shepherd had been a traditional feature of the pastoral elegy since at least the time of Virgil's fifth *Eclogue*. Second, Milton had adhered in all his previous elegies to the established pattern of the Christian *consolatio* with its characteristic progression from mourning to rejoicing.[1] Third, and most important of all, the structural rhythm of the first two movements of the poem, each of which begins in this world and ends in the next, has already prepared us to expect an apocalyptic vision at precisely this juncture of the final movement. However inadequate it may have seemed at the time, Phoebus Apollo's discourse on fame, we now realize, prefigured the "large recompense" which Edward King enjoys in the "blest Kingdoms meek" (177).

Most readers find the Christian fulfilment considerably more satisfying than its pagan adumbration—not, I suspect, because it is better doctrine but simply because it is better poetry:

> So Lycidas sunk low, but mounted high,
> Through the dear might of him that walk'd the waves
> Where other groves, and other streams along,
> With Nectar pure his oozy Locks he laves,
> And hears the unexpressive nuptial Song,
> In the blest Kingdoms meek of joy and love.
> There entertain him all the Saints above,
> In solemn troops, and sweet Societies
> That sing, and singing in their glory move,
> And wipe the tears for ever from his eyes. (172-81)

Whereas Phoebus' speech failed to offer any genuine solace for the frustration of the homely slighted shepherd's sexual and poetic aspirations, this second account of divine reward restores the dead swain to an idealized landscape in which both impulses can be satisfied, albeit vicariously. The "blest Kingdoms meek," that is to say, are characterized by two qualities which were conspicuous by their absence in Jove's bleak court:[2] "joy and love," joy expressed in the singing of the "sweet Societies," love in the "nuptial" union they are celebrating. For Lycidas, as the poem's original readers would have needed no reminding, is attending the marriage of the lamb described in the Book of Revelation:

> And I heard the voice of harpers harping with their harps: And they sung as it were a new song before the throne, and before the four beasts, and the elders: and no man could learn that song but the hundred and forty and four thousand, which were redeemed from the earth. These are they which were not defiled with women; for they are virgins. These are they which follow the Lamb whithersoever he goeth. These were redeemed from among men, ... And I heard as it were the voice of a great multitude, and as the voice of mighty thunderings, saying Alleluia! for the Lord God omnipotent reigneth. Let us be glad and rejoice, and give honour to him: for the marriage of the Lamb is come, and his wife hath made herself ready.[3]

From his late youth to his early middle age, Milton was evidently haunted by these verses—he alludes to them in the *Elegia Tertia* (1626), *At a Solemn Music* (1633), *Ad Patrem* (1637), *Epitaphium Damonis* (1640), *Reason of Church Government* (1642) and *Apology for Smectymnuus* (1642) as well as in *Lycidas*.[4] The reason they touched him so deeply, I believe, was not only that they described the celestial prototype of the "glorious and lofty Hymns" which he himself aspired to compose[5] but also that they furnished scriptural authority for his faith in the sanctifying power of virginity. No one who has been "defiled with women," St. John appeared to confirm, could hope to sing the "new song" honouring the heavenly bridegroom and his bride. What the elder brother called in *Comus* "the arms of chastity" (439) were an essential part of both the poet's and the saint's moral equipment.

At this point it may well be objected that in the *Apology for Smectymnuus* Milton took a rather different view of the matter. "Nor did I slumber over that place expressing such high rewards of ever accompanying the Lambe, with those celestiall songs to others inapprehensible," he assured his readers, "but not to those who were not defil'd with women, which doubtlesse meanes fornication: For mariage must not be call'd a defilement."[6] But although the final reservation in favour of holy matrimony undoubtedly represents the orthodox Protestant interpretation of St. John's anti-feminist sentiments,[7] there is no reason to believe that Milton adopted that interpretation until he himself was on the verge of marriage with Mary Powell in 1642.[8] On the contrary, all the evidence suggests that as late as 1640 he followed Tertullian, Jerome, and Ribera in believing that "by the undefiled [the author of the Apocalyse] understandeth such as have no wives."[9] Certainly, the conclusion of the *Epitaphium Damonis* seems to assume that the evangelist was advocating nothing less than life-long celibacy:

> Because the crimson flush of modesty and youth without stain were your pleasure, because you ne'er tasted the joys of the marriage couch, see! virginal honours are reserved for you. With your bright head encircled by a radiant crown, and carrying the gladsome shade of the bread-leaved palm, you will consummate, eternally, immortal nuptials, where there is singing, where the lyre revels madly, mingled with choirs beatific, and festal orgies run riot, in bacchante fashion, with the thyrsus of Zion. (212-19)

If these lines are any indication of the way in which Milton apprehended St. John's vision when he was writing *Lycidas* just three years earlier, then the apotheosis of Edward King takes on a significant new dimension. For behind the description of Damon's rapture in the *Epitaphium* lies not only the biblical account of the marriage of the lamb but also the neo-Platonic conception of the soul's union with God as a celestial bacchanal. "The spirit of the god Dionysius," wrote Marsilio Ficino:

> was believed by the ancient theologians and Platonists to be the ecstasy and abandon of disencumbered minds, when partly by innate *love*, partly at the instigation of the god, they transgress the natural limits of intelligence and are miraculously transformed into the beloved god himself: where, inebriated by a certain new draft of *nectar* and by an immeasurable *joy*, they rage, as it were, in a bacchic frenzy.[10]

In view of Milton's well-documented interest in neo-Platonic philosophy during his residence at Horton, it seems entirely plausible that the joy and love experienced by Edward King in *Lycidas* are closely related to the kind of Dionysiac ecstasy which Ficino describes in the passage above and which Damon clearly enjoys at the end of Milton's elegy.[11]

The most persuasive evidence in support of this hypothesis, however, is internal rather than external. For Milton's description of Lycidas

among the saints is not simply a Christian fulfilment of the scene originally adumbrated by Phoebus Apollo. It is also a celestial re-enactment of
the events which took place still earlier in the poem on the banks of the
Hebrus. The apotheosis of Lycidas, that is to say, bears a striking resemblance to the death of Orpheus at the hands of the Ciconian women.
Orpheus' gory visage "down the stream was sent" (62); Lycidas washes
his oozy locks "other streams along" (174). Orpheus' head was carried
to "the Lesbian shore" (63); Lycidas will henceforth serve as "the
Genius of the shore" (183). Orpheus was killed by "the rout that made
the hideous roar" (61) because he resisted marriage; Lycidas is enter-
tained by "solemn troops, and sweet Societies" singing a "nuptial Song"
(176-79). The scene in heaven thus reads like a transcendent version
(or, rather, inversion) of the scene in Thrace, harmonizing its disso-
nance, sublimating its violence, reviving its protagonist. In the final
analysis, it is the resurrection of Lycidas rather than the intervention of
Phoebus that dispels the horror of Orpheus' death.

The close connection between these two Bacchic episodes suggests in
turn a rather different way of looking at the poem's structure as a whole.
In the opening paragraph of this chapter my explanation of the reasons
why we may have anticipated an apocalyptic vision at this juncture of
the elegy was based upon the analysis of *Lycidas* which Arthur Barker
worked out during the course of his influential article on the *Nativity
Ode*. Milton's elegy, he argued, consists "of an introduction and conclusion, both pastoral in tone, and three movements, practically equal in
length and precisely parallel in pattern."[12] The first movement (lines
15-84) begins with a lament for the shepherd-poet and ends with
Phoebus' revelation of heavenly fame; the second (lines 85-131) begins
with a lament for the shepherd-priest and ends with St. Peter's promise
of heavenly justice; and the third (lines 132-85) begins with a lament
for the poet-priest and ends with Milton's vision of King's apotheosis.

Ever since Barker published his analysis in 1940 it has been generally
accepted that the basic structure of *Lycidas* is tripartite. Jon S. Lawry,
Marjorie H. Nicolson, Balachandra Rajan, Wayne Shumaker, and A. S.
P. Woodhouse, to name only a few, all take it virtually for granted that
between the prologue and the epilogue the poem develops in three clearly
distinguishable phases. The parallels in imagery and phraseology between
the death of Orpheus and the rebirth of Lycidas, however, disclose an
essentially bipartite structure underlying the tripartite scheme. At this
deeper level, the poem consists, I believe, of two contrasting movements,
the first of which (lines 1-69) is linked to the second (lines 70-193) by

61

an extraordinarily consistent set of thematic, verbal, and iconic correspondences.

.Thus, the major theme of the opening lines (1-22) of the first movement is Milton's premature assault upon his own poetic talent. The theme of the opening lines (70-107) of the second movement is the blind fury's premature assault upon Lycidas. Just as Milton shattered the leaves before the mellowing year, so Atropos slit the young poet's life before his labours came to fruition. In addition to this basic parallel there are numerous details which relate the two sections to each other. The laurel of Apollo in the first line has its counterpart in the plant of fame that grows and spreads aloft in paradise. The "meed" (14) which Milton proposes to offer Lycidas foreshadows the promise of heavenly "meed" (84) in the second passage. The "sacred well" (15) corresponds

TABLE OF CORRESPONDENCES

First Movement	*Second Movement*
1-22	70-107
Milton plucks berries	Atropos plucks Lycidas
Laurels (Apollo)	Plant of Fame (Apollo)
Meed of some melodious tear	Heavenly meed
Sacred well	Fountain Arethuse
Loudly sweep the string	Higher mood
Gentle Muse	Gentle swain
Watry bear, parching wind	Level brine, felon winds
Sable shrowd	Mantle hairy
23-36	108-131
Ideal shepherds' life	Corrupt shepherds' life
Batt'ning our flocks	The hungry Sheep not fed
Fresh dews of night	The rank mist
Rural ditties,	Lean and flashy songs,
Oaten flute	Scrannel pipes
Satyrs and fauns	The grim Woolf
37-49	132-153
Never must return	Return Sicilian Muse
Landscape mourns death	Landscape mourns death

50-57	154-164
Death by water	Death by water
Remorseless deep	Sounding Seas
Anglesey	Hebrides
Mona high	St. Michael's Mount
The famous Druids	Bellerus old
Shaggy top	Bottom of the world

58-63	165-185
Dionysiac revels	Dionysiac revels
Down the stream	Other streams along
Goary visage	Oozy Locks
Lesbian shore	Genius of the shore
The rout	Sweet Societies
The hideous roar	Nuptiall Song
Death	Resurrection

64-69	186-193
Homely slighted Shepherd	Uncouth Swain
Uncessant care	Eager thought
Despair, death	Hope, new beginning

to the "Fountain Arethuse" (85), the "gentle Muse" (19) who may one day mourn for Milton gives way to the "gentle swain" (92) whom Milton is mourning, and the vision of Lycidas' body floating on "his watry bear" (12) and weltering "to the parching wind" (13) is balanced by the bleak seascape of "Waves" and "Fellon Winds" (91). By the same token, the "Sisters" (15) of the sacred well look forward to Panope and "all her sisters" (99) playing on the level brine, while the injunction to "somewhat loudly sweep the string" (17) anticipates the "higher mood" (87) of Phoebus' speech.

The next section of the first movement (lines 23-36) describes the ideal pastoral life which the poet enjoyed with Lycidas before his death. Like faithful herdsmen, they fed their flock with the "fresh dews of night" (29), sang "Rural ditties" (32) accompanied on the "Oaten Flute" (33), and inspired the innocent fauns and satyrs to dance to their music. In the corresponding section of the second movement (lines 108-31), on the contrary, St. Peter denounces the corrupt pastoral life of the faithless herdsmen whose sheep are "not fed" (125) but "swoln with wind, and the rank mist they draw, Rot inwardly" (126). The songs of these intruders, far from being musical, are "lean and flashy" (123), grating on their "scrannel Pipes of wretched straw" (124). No longer are their companions the fauns and satyrs with "clov'n heel" (34) but the grim wolf with his "privy paw" (128).

At this point in both movements the everyday details of the homely slighted shepherd's trade give way to an elaborate description of a flowery landscape which responds sympathetically to Lycidas' death. In lines 37-49 of the first movement the plants mourn spontaneously. In lines 132-53 of the second movement, on the other hand, they have to be summoned to decorate the "Laureat Herse" (151) containing the shepherd's body. The latter passage may "serve no function whatsoever in either the narrative or the logical structure of the poem,"[14] as Clay Hunt asserts, but it serves an absolutely crucial one in what may be called the imagistic structure of *Lycidas*. For without the catalogue of flowers, the symmetry between the two movements would collapse.

Both pastoral interludes are now interrupted by a hideous vision of death by water. In lines 50-57 Milton describes how the "remorseless deep" (50) closed over the head of Lycidas, and reproaches the local nymphs for deserting their customary haunts on "Mona high," the home of "the famous Druids" (53-54). In lines 154-64 he imagines Lycidas' bones being carried by the "sounding Seas" to more distant lands, either north to the "stormy Hebrides" or south to the "guarded Mount" of St. Michael, associated with another piece of Celtic folklore, "the fable of Bellerus old" (160).

By far the most significant and suggestive of these parallels, however, is the final one. For the symmetries I have been tracing point towards a culminating correspondence which overshadows all the rest: the uncouth swain "With eager thought warbling his Dorick lay" in lines 186-93 is the structural equivalent of the homely slighted shepherd questioning the "uncessant care" of his calling in lines 64-69. As the bitterness and despair of the first passage give way to the hope and energy of the second, we sense that here, if anywhere, Milton has come to terms with the anxieties which Phoebus Apollo had so conspicuously failed to dispel. Simply by persisting in his trade, by accepting the possible futility of his labours and pursuing them regardless, the uncouth swain has offered a response to the anguished questions he had posed in his song. Even if it "boots" nothing to meditate the thankless muse, he will still continue to serve her. Just as Lycidas himself has risen from his watery grave, so his companion now seems to undergo a kind of resurrection—"At last he rose, and twitch'd his Mantle blew"—and we are left with the vision of a man, reinvigorated and reassured, setting out like Adam and Eve at the end of *Paradise Lost* for "fresh Woods, and Pastures new" (193). It is in this image of human indomitability that some of the deepest tensions of the poem are resolved, or, if not resolved, overcome by an act of poetic faith.

CHAPTER NINE

Pastures New

The last eight lines of *Lycidas*, Paul Alpers has remarked, "could be the conclusion of almost any eclogue."[1] They have reminded many critics of the conclusion of Virgil's tenth *Eclogue* in particular:

> These strains, Muses divine, it will be enough for your poet to have sung, while he sits idle and twines a basket of slender hibiscus. These ye shall make of highest worth in Gallus' eyes—Gallus, for whom my love grows hour by hour as fast as in the dawn of spring shoots up the green alder. Let us rise; the shade oft brings peril to singers. The juniper's shade brings peril; hurtful to the corn, too, is the shade. Get ye home, my full-fed goats—the Evening-star comes—get ye home! (70-77)

Commenting on the resemblance between this paragraph and the ending of *Lycidas*, J. H. Hanford observes that "both poems close with eight lines, very similar in spirit, referring to the end of day and the departure of the shepherd,"[2] while M. Y. Hughes notes that in Milton's leave-taking we "surely hear an echo of Virgil's farewell to his Lament for Gallus."[3]

Beneath the superficial similarities between the two passages, however, there lies a radical difference which neither critic mentions: in the *Eclogue*, the voice which brings the elegy to a close is the same one that began it, whereas in *Lycidas* the voice which delivers the concluding *ottava rima* belongs to a totally new speaker, quite distinct from the shepherd who has been mourning the death of Edward King in the previous lines:

> Thus sang the uncouth Swain to th'Okes and rills,
> While the still morn went out with Sandals gray,
> He touch'd the tender stops of various Quills,
> With eager thought warbling his Dorick lay:
> And now the Sun had stretch'd out all the hills,
> And now was dropt into the Western Bay;
> At last he rose, and twitch'd his Mantle blew:
> To morrow to fresh Woods, and Pastures new. (186-93)

As Brooks and Hardy point out in their commentary, "there is no third person section at the beginning of the poem in which the 'uncouth swain' is introduced, and to which this last section recurs."[4] On the contrary, the narrator who abruptly intervenes to pronounce the swain "uncouth" is himself a completely unknown quantity.

Ever since J. C. Ransom first drew critical attention to it in 1933,[5] the anomalous nature of the poem's ending has been widely recognized. Unfortunately, it is often discussed in terms which suggest that nothing more is involved than a last-minute switch from the present tense ("weep," "are," "wonder") to the past ("sang," "touch'd," "twitch'd"). In an attempt to refute Ransom's emphasis on Milton's idiosyncrasy, M. C. Battestin, for instance, reminds us that "authority for shifts in tense form could be found in the eclogues of Virgil."[6] So no doubt it could, but that is not the point. What cannot be found in the eclogues of Virgil, or in the eclogues of any other poet for that matter, is authority for the generic transformation that accompanies the change of tense in the final lines of *Lycidas*. For Milton's unexpected introduction of a third-person narrator at the end of a first-person poem violates one of the oldest and most fundamental covenants governing the writer's relationship with his reader: the implicit understanding that the genre of the work will remain constant, that a play will not turn into an epic half way through, or vice-versa.

The genre of *Lycidas*, the headnote informs us, is a "Monody." The term derives, as Milton certainly knew, from Greek tragedy, where it means an ode sung by a single character.[7] The ensuing tribute to Edward King, we are thus led to expect, will be dramatic in character. And indeed it reads very much like a soliloquy. Up to line 185, that is to say, we seem to be in the presence of a single speaker who is addressing us in the dramatic present. But in line 186 a second, unidentified speaker suddenly emerges from the wings and with a single preterite verb thrusts the original speaker (and his speech) back into the past. A work that began as drama has ended as narrative.[8]

The general effect of this startling shift in the poem's modality is readily apparent. It is to create not only a temporal but an ontological gap between the shepherd who sings for Lycidas and the poet who describes him doing so. The epilogue informs us, in M. H. Abrams' words, that the sentiments we have just overheard were being expressed "not by Milton but by a singer Milton is at considerable pains to identify as someone other than himself."[9] So much is obvious. The question is: why does Milton suppress this information until the poem is almost over? Or, to put it another way, why is there no matching narrative introduction to warn us in advance that the "uncouth swain" is a character in, rather than the author of, the elegy? Because, I would suggest, the distinction between the swain and Milton simply does not obtain at the beginning of *Lycidas*. Initially, at least, the two figures are identical. "In this Monody," the headnote declares, "the Author bewails a learned Friend," and there is nothing in the opening paragraphs to prevent us from taking this announcement quite literally. The voice we hear at the beginning of the poem is, unmistakeably, the voice of John Milton himself, agonizing over his poetic immaturity, showing off his classical learning, recalling with evident nostalgia his days as a student in Cambridge.

As the poem progresses, however, the owner of that voice gradually loses his historical identity and finally turns into a fictional character whose values and attitudes Milton the poet does not necessarily share. The first hint that the mourner may not be a constant factor comes in line 56 when he abruptly corrects himself for reproaching the nymphs: "Ay me, I fondly dream! Had ye bin there—for what could that have don?" Eric Smith goes rather too far, perhaps, when he comments that "the overall movement towards assurance by eliminating the misconceptions obliges us to consider the poet as in control and distinct from the speaker."[10] But the second thoughts do open up a tiny fissure in the mourner's consciousness, a fissure that widens dramatically with the intervention of the god of poetry in line 76: "But not the praise, Phoebus repli'd, and touch'd my trembling ears." Here, as Ransom originally noted, the tense suddenly lapses from the dramatic present to the narrative past. As the experience of lines 1-75 is thrust back into an earlier time plane, a gulf opens up between the speaker who remembers Phoebus' advice and the speaker who only a few lines earlier considered abandoning his vocation. The two figures are still recognizably the same person—the ears that Phoebus touches are "my ears," not "his"—but the second figure, enlightened by the revelations of the god of poetry, speaks from a perspective considerably broader than that of his earlier manifestation.

From this point until the end of St. Peter's speech, the predominantly past tenses—"came" (90), "ask'd" (91), "question'd" (93), "knew" (95), "went" (103), "quoth" (107), "came," "did go" (108), "bore" (110), "shook," "bespake" (112)—freeze the passage of time in the mourner's newly created present while he pauses to recall the speeches of the other visitors. With the invocation to Alpheus and the present imperatives that accompany it—"Return" (132), "call," "bid" (134), "Throw" (139), "purple" (141), "Bring" (142)—the clock starts run-ning again, but almost immediately the identity of the speaker undergoes another transformation: it expands to include an undefined chorus of fellow mourners who share the speaker's "false surmise" (153) and his subsequent disillusion as he remembers the true fate of Lycidas' body. The frail thoughts and moist vows belong now to a multiple consciousness; they are "our"s (153, 159) rather than "mine." And a still more violent change occurs shortly afterwards. At line 165 the speaker dissociates himself from his fellow mourners in a change of viewpoint so extreme that one critic has attributed what follows to a completely different character, St. Michael.[11] But we do not have to introduce an *angelus ex machina* in order to understand what is happening here. The vision of Lycidas' resurrection has detached the speaker so completely from his companions that after addressing them directly in the second person in line 165—"Weep no more, woful Shepherds weep no more"— he is able to refer to them objectively in the third person by line 182: "Now Lycidas the Shepherds weep no more." Spatially as well as temporally, the voice which proclaims Edward King's apotheosis is located at two removes from the voice which announced his death in the opening paragraph.

A yet more radical disjunction awaits us in line 185, however. Once again the tenses change, but as we have already seen, the author and the genre of the poem change with them. In the last and most violent of the reversals which the poem forces us to perform, what we took for fact turns into fiction, and the swain is transformed into a figment of Milton's poetic imagination. The process of "self-objectification," as Lowry Nelson calls it,[12] has reached its climax. The entire poem, one might say, records Milton's emergence from the *persona* of the uncouth swain. *Lycidas* is one long act of disengagement.

Critics have reacted to this phenomenon in a variety of ways. Some, like Robert Graves, Kenneth Muir, and E. M. W. Tillyard,[13] ignore the concluding distinction between the swain and the poet and read *Lycidas* in purely autobiographical terms, thereby laying themselves open to the objection urged by M. H. Abrams that Milton clearly distinguishes himself from the swain in the final lines.[14] Others, like Barbara H. Smith, David Berkeley, and D. M. Friedman, ignore the initial identification of the two figures and treat the swain as a dramatic *persona* from the very beginning. Discussing the relation of the elegist to Milton, Smith, for instance, observes: "As always, I am speaking here of the fictional person whose utterance the poem represents. And Milton himself, by introducing a framing conclusion evidently written by someone other than 'the uncouth Swain', certainly emphasizes this fiction."[15] As I have tried to show above, however, the uncouth swain does not *become* fictional until the end of the poem. At the beginning, he is the historical fact we know as John Milton. And while it is certainly legitimate to reinterpret the earlier sections of the poem retrospectively in the light of what we learn later—indeed, as we have seen, Milton's method is to force us to do so repeatedly—it is not legitimate to read the poem as if we knew from the very outset that the uncouth swain was a fictional *persona*. If that is how Milton intended us to respond, he would have supplied a balancing prologue. To say, with Friedman, that "Milton chose a pastoral *persona*"[16] through which to speak *Lycidas* is to be wise before the event.

Recently, Berkeley has carried this view of the speaker still further in an analysis of *Lycidas* which depicts the swain as a fully-fledged fictional character with whom Milton has nothing whatever in common. After reprimanding Muir for confusing "the swain as *persona* with the proper voice of the author,"[17] he characterizes the former as "an unknowledgeable pagan" who utters "thoughts beyond his thoughts," a naive mouthpiece for religious typologies which he himself does not understand or intend.[18] Quite apart from its inherent improbability—why would a Christian scholar choose an ignorant heathen to be his spokesman in a tribute to a learned friend destined for the ministry?—this interpretation of the poem is flawed by its failure to recognize the intensely personal force of the questions Milton poses as he contemplates the implications of King's death. For as Fish observes, "here is no mediated pastoral voice, heard through a screen of tradition and ritual; here is the thing itself, the expression of a distinctive perspective on a problem that others may have considered . . . but never with such poignancy and perceptiveness."[19]

At the opposite extreme from Berkeley, Clay Hunt argues in his study of *Lycidas* and the Italian critics that Milton is to be associated exclusively with the swain. It is the voice speaking the *ottava rima*, according to Hunt, that belongs to a *persona*. Commenting on line 185 he writes: "At this point a new speaker takes over, someone not involved with Milton's personal feelings about King's death, who looks on the scene from the outside. As he coolly describes Milton in the act of spending an entire day . . . writing the poem, he detaches us from all personal feeling the poem has expressed."[20] The effect of the epilogue, then, is to provide "a final impression of the poem as performance," in Nelson's words,[21] to insulate the experience it contains from any direct contact with the real world.

Divergent as they are, all these readings share one fundamental assumption, the notion that "*Lycidas* is the expression of a unified consciousness."[22] From which it follows, of course, that if the swain is Milton then the voice at the end must belong to someone else, and vice-versa. It seems to me, on the contrary, that *Lycidas* is the expression of a consciousness that grows increasingly divided as the poem progresses until at line 186 the second self becomes completely independent of the first. I cannot quite agree with Louis L. Martz, therefore, when he states that "Milton at the close reveals the presence of the mature consciousness that has guided the words of his 'uncouth swain' throughout the poem."[23] For "the mature consciousness" of the final *ottava rima* has only come into being, I believe, during the course of the elegy. It is not that the author has concealed himself behind the pastoral scenery in order to make a surprise appearance at the end. It is, rather, that the poem has acquired a new author, that Milton has undergone a transformation so profound that by the end of the poem he has become, quite literally, another person. Far from being "in control of the poem's diction from the very beginning," as Friedman asserts,[24] the voice we hear in the *ottava rima* did not exist at the beginning of the poem.

The conclusion of *Lycidas* thus enacts in an extraordinarily vivid way an experience analogous to, though not, I think, identical with, the Christian conversion experience. Fish describes it in terms of the disappearance of the speaker from the scene of his own poem,[25] but there is rather more involved here than a mere disappearance. For as the old speaker fades away, a new speaker is born. Like a snake sloughing its skin, the singer withdraws from his song and in the final lines begins what is essentially a new song which contains the old one. It is as if the self of a dream had suddenly awakened into the self of everyday reality. The elegy and the swain who sang it recede into the distance, and we are left with the sense that we have witnessed a rebirth. In Pauline terms, Milton has cast off the old man to put on the new.

But who is this new man, and what does he represent? As is so often the case with Milton's poetry, the verse-form itself holds the key. The concluding eight lines of *Lycidas* are in *ottava rima*, the major vehicle of narrative poetry in the Renaissance. As Martz notes, therefore, there is "a special decorum in this concluding metrical form," for just as Milton shifts into a "stanza that is best known for objective narration" so "the mode of the poem shifts to the third person."[26] Still more to the point, *ottava rima* was associated not just with narrative verse in general but with a particular kind of narrative verse. It was the standard vehicle of the sixteenth-century romantic epic, the stanza of Tasso's *Gerusalemme Liberata*, Ariosto's *Orlando Furioso*, and of their English translations by Fairfax and Harington. As the verse form in which the amorous and military conquests of Roland and Godfrey has been celebrated, the *ottava rima* thus implies a great deal more than "objective narration." It invokes the turbulent world of heroic action and romantic love.[27] The concluding stanza of *Lycidas* thus carries with it a set of values diametrically opposed to those associated either with the pastoral as a genre or with Edward King as a character. After the meditative, loosely organized, *canzoni* preceding it, it acts like a sudden burst of adrenalin, rousing the singer from his reverie and propelling him towards the wars of truth in which "the true warfaring Christian" could show his mettle. The new verse form thus opens up the possibility of living an entirely different kind of life, animated no longer by the ideals of the pastoral eclogue but rather by those of the Christian epic. The course of Milton's life, it suggests, is about to undergo a drastic change.

Most critics of the poem would limit that change to the specific area of Milton's literary ambitions. While recognizing the heroic overtones of the final *ottava rima*, they take them to imply no more than a decison, analogous to Virgil's at the end of the tenth *Eclogue*, to abandon the pastoral for the epic. For John Spencer Hill, the conclusion of *Lycidas* is the prelude to "a new dawn of poetic promise"[28] while for Wittreich it signals the entry of vision into the world of action. "His confidence in the power of song buoyed up by the story of Orpheus' success in liberating Eurydice," he writes, "Milton is now ready to unleash his power, his poetry, upon the world."[29] The problem, of course, is that the new day did not break for another thirty years, that for the next two decades Milton chose to unleash his power not in poetry but in prose.

If my reading of the poem is correct, on the other hand, *Lycidas* foreshadows Milton's decision to shelve his poetic ambitions. For as I have already suggested, his confidence in the power of song must have been severely shaken, if not completely subverted, by the questions which the death of Edward King had forced upon him. If songs were powerless in the face of violence and injustice, as Lycidas' namesake had been taught in the ninth *Eclogue* and as the death of Orpheus appeared to confirm, then what was the point of the self-denial which Milton believed was the prerequisite of singing them? Even the apocalyptic vision of Lycidas enjoying the rewards of abstinence in heaven could not entirely dispel the nagging fear that in a cruel and chaotic world it was futile to meditate the thankless muse. And if, as he was to write later, it was "folly to commit anything elaborately composed to the careless and interrupted listening of these tumultuous times,"[30] then surely he should direct his energies to some more useful activity. What is more, as I argued in chapter 7, the abuses identified in St. Peter's speech cried out so desperately for reform that any prolongation of his pastoral retreat had become unthinkable. It was time to lose his political as well as his sexual virginity, "to leave a calm and pleasing solitariness, fed with cheerful and confident thought, to embark in a troubled sea of noises and hoarse disputes."[31] The moral of *Lycidas* is almost the opposite of Voltaire's in *Candide*: "Il faut quitter notre jardin." "To morrow to fresh woods and pastures new."[32]

That much misquoted final line is deceptively simple. After the past tenses of the other verbs in the stanza, it suddenly reverts back into a vague kind of present: "To morrow to . . . " What the grammar does not make clear, however, is just who is planning to set off. Is it the uncouth swain or John Milton? The answer, I would suggest, is both, for despite the disjunction we have analyzed, the uncouth swain is still a part of Milton. We cannot leave our pasts behind us like a landscape; what we have been is still part of what we are. So in the final line of the poem the swain's voice merges with his author's in a declaration that means something different for each of them. In the swain's mouth, as I suggested in chapter 8, it affirms his will to go on, his determination to persist in the homely slighted shepherd's trade despite the death of his friend. In Milton's mouth it announces his departure from the pastoral world and all it stands for. At last he has broken out of the sterile repetitious cycle in which he was trapped in the opening lines. "Yet once more" has given way to "no more" and finally to "fresh woods and pastures new." Whereas in *Ad Patrem* he had declared: "no more shall I mingle, a figure obscure, with the witless populace, but my footsteps will avoid eyes profane" (103-04), now he writes to Charles Diodati: "What am I doing? Growing my wings and meditating flight; but as yet our Pegasus raises himself on very tender pinions."[33] The bird is about to leave the nest.

Like Marvell's *Horatian Ode*, then, *Lycidas* is about an epiphany. No longer content to sing his numbers languishing in the shades of Horton, Milton is about to abandon that part of himself represented by the swain with his devotion to chastity, retirement, and poetry in order to pursue the open-ended future of heroic and erotic engagement which the verse-form has simultaneously invoked. Five years later, at all events, he was doing precisely what Boccaccio and the commentators on Theocritus and Virgil had insisted a poet should not be doing: embroiling himself in the dust and heat of politics and marriage. Despite the ringing declarations of poetic ambition in Book II of *The Reason of Church Government*, the fact is that the world had to wait more than two decades for the appearance of *Paradise Lost*. Not until the dying days of the Commonwealth when he was almost sixty would Milton reassume that part of his identity which he had discarded at the end of *Lycidas* and take up the mantle of the shepherd poet yet once more.

NOTES

NOTES TO INTRODUCTION

[1] Daniel J. Levinson, *The Seasons of a Man's Life* (New York: Ballantine Books, 1979), p. 86.

[2] *Ibid.*, p. 85.

NOTES TO CHAPTER ONE

[1] All quotations from Milton's poetry and prose are from Frank A. Patterson, gen. ed., *The Works of John Milton* (New York: Columbia Univ. Press, 1931-38).

[2] A. S. P. Woodhouse and Douglas Bush, *A Variorum Commentary on the Poems of John Milton*, II, 2 (New York: Columbia Univ. Press, 1972), 652, cited hereafter as *Variorum*.

[3] Line 240.

[4] "The Primary Language of *Lycidas*" in C. A. Patrides, ed., *Milton's Lycidas, The Tradition and the Poem* (New York: Holt, Rinehart, Winston, 1961), pp. 95-100, cited hereafter as Patrides.

[5] Lines 8-9, 15-17, 25-27, 58-59, 132-33, 190-91.

[6] See Rosalie L. Colie, *My Ecchoing Song, Marvell's Poetry of Criticism* (Princeton: Princeton Univ. Press, 1970).

[7] Lines 6-7. I quote throughout from H. Rushton Fairclough's translation of the *Eclogues* in the Loeb Classical Library's revised edition of the works of Virgil, I (London: William Heinemann Ltd., 1967).

[8] Quoted by Joseph A. Wittreich Jr. in his *Visionary Poetics* (San Marino: Huntington Library, 1979), p. 130.

[9] See below, chapter 4.

[10] On the verbal echoes in the entire corpus of Milton's writings see E. S. LeComte, *Yet Once More: Verbal and Psychological Pattern in Milton* (New York: Liberal Arts Press, 1953).

[11] Romans, v. 19.

[12] Although the pattern I have been describing might appear at first sight to have a good deal in common with the pattern of paradox, there is an important difference between them. Paradox is static. The second element in the opposition is an alternative to the first, and the two elements are

held in suspension, each having equal weight. Reversal, on the other hand, is dynamic. The second element in the opposition is a transformation of the first, and far from being held in suspension with it, actually displaces it.

[13] *Op. cit.*, p. 95.

[14] "The Archetypal Pattern of Death and Rebirth in *Lycidas*" in Patrides, pp. 120-25.

[15] *The Anxiety of Influence* (New York: Oxford Univ. Press, 1973), p. 30.

NOTES TO CHAPTER TWO

[1] "Who is Lycidas?", *Yale French Studies*, 47 (1972), 170. In her note "Milton's *Lycidas*: New Light on the Title," *NQ*, 24 (1977), 545, Joanne M. Riley suggests that Lycidas' name is connected with the Greek *lusis* (deliverance, liberation). In fact the name derives, of course, from the Greek *lukis* (wolf) and means "the wolf's son." In view of his use of the wolf in line 128 it seems unlikely, however, that Milton would have wished to remind his readers of this derivation.

[2] *Variorum*, p. 637.

[3] After reviewing Lycidas' appearance in Theocritus' seventh *Idyl*, Virgil's ninth *Eclogue*, and Sannazaro's *Phyllis*, Martz concludes that "the name Lycidas ... prepares us from the outset for the poem's movement beyond the limitations of the pastoral elegy into the broader reaches of the pastoral eclogue with its awareness of the world of history" (*Op. cit.*, p. 187). My analysis will be more concerned with the ironic relationship between Milton's protagonist and his namesakes.

[4] *Awake the Courteous Echo* (Toronto: Univ. of Toronto Press, 1973), p. 91, n. 26.

[5] In his edition, *John Milton: Complete Poems and Major Prose* (New York: Odyssey Press, 1957), p. 136, Merritt Y. Hughes incorrectly states that Menalcas is one of the competitors in *Idyl* VII.

[6] *Virgil's Pastoral Art* (Princeton: Princeton Univ. Press, 1970).

[7] I quote throughout from the translation of Theocritus' *Idyls* in Thomas P. Harrison, *The Pastoral Elegy: An Anthology* (Austin: Univ. of Texas Press, 1939).

[8] On the relationship between Fletcher's elegy and *Lycidas* see W. B. Austin, "Milton's *Lycidas* and Two Latin Elegies by Giles Fletcher the Elder," *SP*, 44 (1947), 41-55.

[9] *Theocritus' Coan Pastorals* (Cambridge, Mass.: Harvard Univ. Press, 1967), p. 10.

[10] See also below, chapter 4. In the pseudo-Theocritean *Idyl* XVIII Daphnis claims that Lycidas is his father. Several recent commentators note an allusion to Virgil's messianic eclogue in Milton's invocation to the muses but miss the allusion to Theocritus, perhaps because J. M. Edmonds'

translation in the Loeb Library edition of Theocritus does not accurately render the Greek.

[11] *Op. cit.*, p. 300.

[12] *Ibid.*, p. 338.

NOTES TO CHAPTER THREE

[1] *Journal of the Warburg and Cortauld Institutes*, 21 (1958), 254.

[2] See, for instance: *Elegia Sexta*, 15-16, *Mansus*, 92.

[3] See the note to lines 1-2 in John Carey and Alastair Fowler, *The Poems of John Milton* (London: Longman's, Green & Co., 1968).

[4] See also the note to lines 1-2 in Thomas Newton, *Paradise Regained, A Poem in Four Books To which is added Samson Agonistes and Poems upon Several Occasions* (London, 1752): "the ivy, as a reward for his learning."

[5] *Mansus*, 92.

[6] *Loc. cit.*

[7] *Variorum*, p. 640.

[8] Columbia, III, i, 241.

[9] "Essays in Analysis: *Lycidas*" in Patrides, p. 137. By the same token, of course, the transfiguration of those shattered leaves into a fully mature and articulate song parallels the apotheosis of its subject.

[10] "*Lycidas*: the Swain's Paideia," *Milton Studies*, 3 (1971), 7-8.

[11] The phrase occurs in Milton's letter to Charles Diodati dated September 2, 1637 (Columbia, XII, 19).

NOTES TO CHAPTER FOUR

[1] Clay Hunt, for instance, writes in his *Lycidas and the Italian Critics* (New Haven: Yale Univ. Press, 1979), p. 129: "The first section of the poem proper, the dirge for Lycidas, begins at line 15 with the invocation to the classical Muses to 'begin'." Cf. Stanley E. Fish, "*Lycidas*: A Poem Finally Anonymous," *Glyph*, 8 (1981), 6.

[2] "The Pastoral Elegy and Milton's *Lycidas*" in Patrides, pp. 27-55.

[3] I quote from the summary of Gebauer's thesis which R. M. Ogilvie provides during the course of his vigorous attempt to refute it in his article "The Song of Thyrsis," *Journal of Hellenic Studies*, 82 (1962), 107.

[4] In Virgil's *Eclogue* X, 21, the shepherds put a similar question to a lover who really is in this predicament.

[5] Thomas Stanley, trans., *Claudius Aelianus His Various History* (London, 1666), p. 203, quoted by Ellen Z. Lambert in *Placing Sorrow: A Study of the Pastoral Convention from Theocritus to Milton* (Chapel Hill:

Univ. of North Carolina Press, 1976), p. xxxii. Lambert believes that this version of the myth can be made to fit the facts of Theocritus' first *Idyl* by assuming that the passion for which Daphnis is wasting away is either for the princess, in which case the nymph is searching for him, or for the nymph, in which case the princess is searching for him. Neither alternative seems to me very convincing. Priapus' comment would be pointless if the woman for whom Daphnis is pining away were not the same as the woman who is searching for him.

6 *Theocritus' Coan Pastorals*, p. 25. Cf. A. S. F. Gow, *Theocritus* (Cambridge: Cambridge Univ. Press, 1952), II, 1.

7 Lambert believes that "Gallus does not go to his death but simply yields to his passions" (p. 45), while Paul Alpers suggests in *The Singer of the Eclogues* (Berkeley: Univ. of California Press, 1979) that Gallus' death is "purely metaphoric" (p. 223). Virgil specifically states in line 10, however, that Gallus was "perishing" (*peribat*) of his love.

8 See, for example: Davis P. Harding, *Milton and the Renaissance Ovid* (Urbana: Univ. of Illinois Press, 1946); Don Cameron Allen, *Mysteriously Meant* (Baltimore: The Johns Hopkins Press, 1970).

9 The annotations of all three are reprinted in Daniel Heinsius' *Theocriti, Moschi, Simii quae extant: cum Graecis in Theocritum Scholiis & Indice copiose,...Accedunt Iosephi Scaligeri, Isaaci Casauboni, & eiusdem Danielis Heinsii Notae & Lectiones* (Heidelberg, 1604).

10 *Theocriti Idyllium Primum Annotationibus Frederici Lamotii illustratum* (Paris, 1552).

11 *Ioannis Meursi ad Theocriti Syracusani Poetae Idyllia Spicilegium* (London, 1597).

12 *Seriatim: Theocritus scripsit Philethicus Latihum* [*sic*] *fecit Bucolicum Carmen Res Acta Syracusis* (Rome, c. 1480); *Theocriti Syracusani eidyllia trigintasex, Latino carmine reddita, Helio Eobano Hesso interprete* Basel, 1531); *Theocriti Syracusani Opera Latine a Ioanne Trimanino ad verbum diligentissime expressa, locis unde Virgilius sumpsit, indicatis* (Venice, 1539); *Theocriti Syracusani poetae Clarissimi idyllia trigintasex, recens a graeco in latinum, ad verbum translata, Andrea Divo Iustinopolitano interprete* (Basel, 1554); *Moschi, Bionis, Theocriti, Elegantissimorum poetarum idyllia aliquot, ab Henrico Stephano Latina facta* (Venice, 1555); Hieronumus Commelinus, *Theocriti Syracusii Idyllia & Epigrammata* (Heidelberg, 1596).

13 I quote both Mancinelli and Ascensius from the following edition: *P. Virgilii Maronis Opera...cum xi acerrimi iudicii virorum commentariis* (Venice, 1544).

14 *Seriatim: Opera Vergiliana* (n.p., 1528); *Io Lodovico Vivis in Bucolica Vergilii Interpretatio, Potissimum Allegorica* (Milan, 1539); "Eclogae decem, cum Annotationibus et castigatione Helii Hessi, et al." in *Publii Vergilii Maronis Mantuani Opera* (London, 1535); *P. Virgilii Maronis*

Bucolica Cum Commentariis Richardi Gorraei Parisiensis (Venice, 1554);
*Argumenta seu Dispositiones Rhetoricae in Eclogas Virgilii Authore
Philip Melanchthon* (n.p., 1568); *Paraphrases, Ecphrases, succintae ques-
tiones, & brevia Scholia Textus in easdam Eclogas Authore M. Stephano
Riccio* (n.p., 1568); *P. Virgilii Maronis Bucolica P. Rami Professoris
Regii, praelectionibus exposita,* 4th ed. (Frankfurt, 1582); *Publi Virgilii-
Maronis Bucolica, Georgica, Aeneis, Notis admarginalibus illustrata a
Thoma Farnabio* (London, 1634).

15 In his *Poems upon Several Occasions* (London, 1791) Thomas Warton
warns us not to confuse King's schoolmaster with the "celebrated rhetori-
cian" (p. 37), but the *DNB* does not distinguish between them.

16 In fact, Fleming made two attempts, the first in fourteener couplets
(1575), the second, from which I quote, in unrhymed fourteeners: *The
Bucolicks of Publius Virgilius Maro ... All newly translated into English
verse by A[braham] F[leming]* (London, 1589).

17 *Seriatim: Virgil's Eclogues ... Translated Grammatically* (London,
1620); *Virgil's Ecologues Translated into English by W. L. Gent.* (London, 1628); *Virgil's Bucolicks Englished* (London, 1634).

18 Fleming also claimed that his 1575 translation was made "for the benefit
of young learners of the latine tongue."

19 *Op. cit.*, p. 29. Cf. Melanchthon, sig. G7: "It is written in imitation of
Theocritus first Idyl concerning Daphnis."

20 "Scholae Theocritae" in Heinsius, p. 302. I am indebted to Professor
A. G. Rigg throughout for his help in translating the commentators'
Latin.

21 *Theocriti Syracusani eidyllia trigintasex*, sig. a8ᵛ. The borrowing establishes Daphnis' love as "indignus."

22 The translations of Heinsius and Scaliger are contained in the former's
reissue of Commelinus' *Theocriti Syracusii Idyllia* (Heidelberg, 1603),
pp. 128-31. Daniel Alsworth's was published in his *Imitatio Theocritea
Qua Virgilii Eclogae, ita Doricis versibus exprimuntur* (Rome, 1594).

23 *Dictionarium Etymologicum Proprium Nominum* (London, 1648), p.
257. See also the passage from Thomas Stanley's translation of Claudius
Aelianus quoted above, pp. oo-o.

24 *Op. cit.*, p. 302. Cf. Lamotius, p. 12: "Suidas says he [Daphnis] was
blinded because he had intercourse with another woman when he was
drunk."

25 *Ibid.*, p. 303. The hapless "Graecus interpres" is a constant target of
Heinsius' editorial barbs.

26 *Ibid.*, p. 304. It was this interpretation of the passage which Heinsius incorporated into the Latin translation of the first *Idyl* which he made for
the 1603 reissue of Commelinus' text: "Puella Per varios fontes pedibus
per devia fertur ... Multa movens: in amore levis nimiumque vagaris ..."

79

But a year later, fearing perhaps that this was not clear or emphatic enough, he revised the translation of line 85 for the 1604 edition to read: "Vocibus his: Levis ah Daphni es, nimiumque vagaris. . . ." The translations of Trimaninus, Divus, and the anonymous translator all render *zateusa* by *quaerens* (seeking), while Hessus prefers *requirens* (searching). It is worth noting also that Heinsius translates *duseros* in line 85 as *levis* (fickle) rather than the more common "poor at loving," thereby anticipating R. M. Ogilvie's point in "The Song of Thyrsis."

[27] *In Vergilii Bucolica et Georgica Commentarii*, ed. G. Thilo (Lipsiae, 1887), p. 118. Cf. Riccius, sig. M7: "Gallus died through the impatience of love [*inpatientia amoris*]."

[28] *The Bukolicks*, p. 29. Cf. Riccius, who throughout his *Brevia et erudita scholia* insists that Gallus was *insanis* (pp. 7ᵛ, 8ᵛ, 9ᵛ), and Hessus, who explains in his comment on lines 31 ff. that "Fingit Gallum respondentem, ut magis ob oculos ponat hominis insaniam" (p. 14ᵛ).

[29] Bidle, sig. C2ᵛ: "Scorcht with Idalian Flames, fond Gallus is Enamour'd on the Strumpet Cytheris." Cf. Melanchthon, sig. G8: "stulti amatoris imago."

[30] *Virgils Eclogues*, p. 92. The phrase is Brinsley's addition to Servius' note.

[31] The phrase runs like a refrain through Riccius' *Brevia et erudita scholia*. It connects Gallus with Daphnis, of whom Heinsius writes: "Obiicitur Daphnidi amoris inconstantia" (p. 303).

[32] *Op. cit.*, sig. M7. Gorraeus agrees, but also approves (p. 154).

[33] *Op. cit.*, p. 98. Cf. Ramus, p. 166. Brinsley evidently knew Ramus' commentary well and did not hesitate to borrow interpretations from it. Cf. sig. A4.

[34] Servius, p. 120. Cf. Lisle, p. 184, Brinsley, p. 95.

[35] *Ibid.*, p. 120. Riccius repeats this phrase word for word without acknowledgement in his *Brevis et erudita scholiae*, p. 5ᵛ.

[36] *P. Virgilii Maronis Opera*, p. 49. See also J. M. Steadman, "Chaste Muse and *Casta Juventus*: Milton, Minturno, and Scaliger on Inspiration and the Poet's Character," *Italica*, 40 (1963), 28-34.

[37] *Op. cit.*, p. 95. Cf. Riccius, p. 5ᵛ, Ramus, p. 161. In his *Erotemata in Decimam Eclogam* sig. Vᵛ Riccius draws the same moral but substitutes philosophy for poetry: "By saying this without doubt he intended to signify only that love, the most powerful of emotions, can be, if not removed, at least assuaged, by excellent precepts drawn from the recondite and hidden points of philosophy."

[38] Melanchton, sig. G8.

[39] I quote from Lisle's translation, p. 11. Cf. Fleming's letter of dedication to his 1589 translation: "The matter or drift of the poet is meere allegoricall, and carrieth another meaning than the litterall interpretation seemeth to afford" (sig. A2ᵛ).

[40] See, for instance, his comment on line 17 of Virgil's *Eclogue* X: "Allegorically this says: nor should you be ashamed to write pastoral poems" (p. 121).

[41] *In Vergilii Bucolica*, p. 118.

[42] Lisle, p. 175, translating Vives, p. 34. Cf. Fleming's "Argument": "How this Gallus was an excellent poet, and so familiar with Caesar, and likewise so favoured of him, that he gave and bestowed upon him the government of Ægypt. Howbeit afterwards growing in suspicion of conspiracie of treason against Caesar, he was slaine at his commandment" (p. 29). The disagreement as to whether Gallus "killed himselfe" as Lisle believed or "was slaine" as Fleming asserts seems to depend on whether the writer in question interprets Servius' *occisus est* as a passive or a reflexive verb. Melanchthon compromises by claiming that Gallus was ordered to kill himself (sig. G6^r).

[43] Melanchthon, on the contrary, appears to cast Gallus as Lycoris and Caesar as Gallus: "I think that secretly the discord which had arisen between Antony and Augustus is being lamented. For Gallus was very close to both" (sig. G6^r).

[44] Lisle, p. 184, translating Vives, p. 34. Cf. Riccius' *Ecphrasis*: "For I have no doubt that if Gallus had persevered in the study of poetry he would not have desired the friendship of the powerful to such an extent nor undertaken those affairs which brought him to his death" (sig. M8^v).

[45] Lisle, pp. 187-88, translating Vives, p. 35^v. Cf. Melanchthon: "This signifies that a private life is sweeter than the administration of the Republic" (sig. G6^v); Riccius: "Would that I had stayed in studies of letters and in private life, or had been erudite" (sig. N^r).

[46] Lisle, p. 187, translating Vives, p. 35^v.

[47] Sig. N^v.

[48] *Argumenta*, sig. G6^r. Only the first of Melanchthon's analyses treats the poem in allegorical terms. The remaining five are rigorously literal.

[49] Revelation, xiv, xix. See below, chapter 8.

NOTES TO CHAPTER FIVE

[1] Both are named, however, in two closely associated poems, Daphnis in *Epitaphium Damonis*, 1, 31, and Gallus in *Mansus*, 4.

[2] See, for instance, *Claudius Aelianus*, p. 203: "[Daphnis] had this name from an accident: for he was born of a nymph and as soon as born exposed under a laurel tree."

[3] "The Orpheus Image in *Lycidas*," PMLA, 64 (1949), 189.

[4] *Seriatim*: "Spenser and the Renaissance Orpheus," *UTQ*, 41 (1971), 24-47; "The Young Milton, Orpheus, and Poetry," *English Studies*, 59 (1978), 27-34; *Orpheus in the Middle Ages* (Cambridge, Mass.: Har-

vard Univ. Press, 1970); *The Untuning of the Sky* (Princeton: Princeton Univ. Press, 1961); "Orpheus: the Neoclassic Vision" in *Opera as Drama* (New York: Knopf, 1956); "Orpheus the Theologian and Renaissance Platonists," *Journal of the Warburg and Cortauld Institutes*, 16 (1953), 100-20; "The Myth of Orpheus in *L'Allegro* and *Il Penseroso*," *MLQ*, 32 (1971), 377-86.

5 *Seriatim*: "The Archetypal Pattern of Death and Rebirth in *Lycidas*" in Patrides, pp. 120-25; "Approaches to *Lycidas*" in Frank Kermode, *The Living Milton* (London: Routledge & Kegan Paul, 1960), pp. 32-54; "Literature as Context: Milton's *Lycidas*" in Patrides, pp. 200-11; "Theme, Pattern, and Imagery in *Lycidas*" in Patrides, pp. 167-200.

6 "The Orpheus Image," pp. 190-91. In a footnote Mayerson observes that Milton "followed Ovid's account most closely."

7 *Poems upon Several Occasions*, note to line 58. Here, perhaps, is the source of what might be called the "hydraulic" interpretation of *Lycidas*, according to which water, in its destructive and redemptive aspects, is one of the poem's most important symbols. As the editors of the *Variorum Commentary* point out, however, Warton's comment is not quite accurate; Orpheus died of dismemberment, not by drowning.

8 "Theme, Pattern, and Imagery," p. 185.

9 Mayerson, p. 202.

10 Adams, p. 124.

11 "Approaches to *Lycidas*," p. 40.

12 My own critical method in this monograph, I realize, also draws attention both to the resemblances and to the differences between Edward King and the various figures Milton compares him with. My objection to Fraser's analysis is that he does not discriminate between the two kinds of relationship.

13 Medieval commentators, however, were more sensitive to the elementary laws of logic than some of their modern successors. Confronted by the differences between Christ and Orpheus noted by Fraser, Pierre Bersuire, for example, attempted to bring the pagan legend into conformity with Christian teaching by giving it a happy ending; in his *Metamorfosis Ovidiana moraliter explanata* (1342) Orpheus succeeds in bringing Eurydice back from the underworld. In the seventeenth century, on the other hand, Alexander Ross made the contrast between the two quests the occasion for affirming Christ's superiority. "What was in vain attempted by Orpheus," he declared in his *Mystagogus Poeticus* (London, 1647), p. 339, "was performed by our Saviour, for he alone hath delivered our soules from the nethermost hell."

14 This shift in emphasis was facilitated by the fact that Ovid had split the story into two separate sections in his *Metamorphoses*. Orpheus' descent into the underworld is related in Book X, his subsequent adventures in Book XI.

[15] "Spenser and the Renaissance Orpheus," p. 25.

[16] Cf. *The Merchant of Venice*, V. i. 79-82.

[17] Giles Fletcher's treatment of the story in *Christ's Victory and Triumph* is unusual in preserving the medieval christological version of the myth.

[18] *Op. cit.*, p. 194. Of the four episodes in Orpheus' life which, according to Cain, were most often treated by the Humanists, none includes the Bacchantes' assault. Interestingly enough, it is this final section of the legend that Milton's nephew, Edward Phillips, emphasizes in his account of Orpheus' life in *The New World of English Words* (London, 1658).

[19] Cain, p. 25.

[20] In the view of the parallels in phraseology with *Lycidas*, the later date seems to me more probable.

[21] Cf. Warton's note to line 176.

[22] See above, chapter 2. Marilyn Williamson finds an analogous difference in the use of the myth in *L'Allegro* and *Il Penseroso*.

[23] *Metamorphoses*, X. 79 - XI. 43. I quote from M. M. Innes' translation in the Penguin edition (London, 1955). Cf. Virgil, *Georgics*, IV. 507-27.

[24] *Op. cit.*, p. 190.

[25] *Op. cit.*, p. 657. Cf. Eric Smith's observation in *By Mourning Tongues: Studies in English Elegy* (Ipswich: Boydell Press, 1977), p. 27, that Orpheus was killed "by the Bacchantes in jealousy of his faithfulness to his dead wife Eurydice."

[26] *Consolation of Philosophy*, III. 12. Cf. Salutati's interpretation of the story, quoted in Friedman, p. 88, n. 60.

[27] Quoted in Friedman, p. 123.

[28] Quoted in Friedman, p. 120. With the notable exception of Golding, Renaissance commentators tended to ignore Orpheus' homosexuality.

[29] Quoted in Cain, pp. 26-27.

[30] Bacon, *Wisdom of the Ancients*, XI, quoted from J. Spedding et al., *Sir Francis Bacon: The Works* (Boston: Brown and Taggard, 1860-64), VI, 172.

[31] *Ovid's Metamorphoses Englished, Mythologiz'd and Represented in Figures* (Oxford, 1632), p. 387.

[32] See under "Orpheus" in *Dictionarium Historicum et Poeticum* (London, 1565). The idea that Orpheus preached against marriage seems to have been a medieval addition to the story. See Friedman, p. 171.

[33] Interestingly enough, Orpheus was directly associated with Gallus in at least two Renaissance commentaries. According to Servius, Virgil had originally concluded his fourth *Georgic* with a eulogy to his fellow poet, but was ordered by Caesar Augustus to omit it when Gallus fell from

favour in 26 B.C. In its place Virgil inserted the fable of Aristaeus, which culminates in the Orpheus episode. By the sixteenth century Servius' anecdote was taken to mean that Virgil had simply substituted a covert for an overt tribute to Gallus, praising him, in Melanchthon's words, "sub fabula Aristei" (fol. G7). Cf. Abraham Fleming, p. 29.

[34] Brinsley, p. 95.

[35] The phrase creates another link between Theocritus' first *Idyl* and *Lycidas*.

[36] *Loc. cit.*

NOTES TO CHAPTER SIX

[1] *Milton, Mannerist and Baroque* (Toronto: Univ. of Toronto Press, 1963), p. 39. Among the other evidence to which Daniells refers is the well known passage in *Paradise Lost*, III. 32-38.

[2] Milton's imagination seems to have been fascinated by underground rivers. Cf. his description of the Tigris in *Paradise Lost*, IX. 69-73.

[3] The Muse in *Lycidas* is "thankless" not, as some critics have suggested, because she receives no thanks but because she offers none to her adherents.

[4] *Volpone*, III. vii. 165-66.

[5] In his article "The Development of the Flower Passage in *Lycidas*," *MLN*, 45 (1950), 468-72, H. H. Adams argues that Milton revised these lines because he realized that the "sensual" overtones he had given the image of the primrose were "completely inappropriate." It seems to me, nevertheless, that the original version of the passage provides interesting evidence concerning Milton's state of mind while he was writing the poem. At this point of his life he seems to have been especially sensitive to the pathos of "uninjoyed love." Cf. his reference in the *Elegia Prima* to the "puer infelix" who "leaves joys untasted, and falls in death ... through the rending of his love" (41-42), and his description in the *Epitaphium Damonis* of the "unwedded" grapes which wither with "their clusters neglected" (65).

[6] *Yet Once More*, p. 6.

[7] Cf. the simultaneous allusions in the title and the address to the nymphs.

[8] J. M. French argues in his article on "The Digressions in Milton's *Lycidas*," *SP*, 50 (1953), 485-90, that there is also a structural parallel between Milton's questions here and St. Peter's attack on the clergy." "Amaryllis," he writes, "has been metamorphosed into ecclesiastical sinecure but the principle is the same."

[9] See above, chapter 5. In *Paradise Lost*, as several commentators have noted, the process of poetic inspiration is described in terms that suggest the act of insemination. E. C. LeComte has also noted a "sly equation

between poetic inspiration and male potency in the *Elegia V* ("Sly "Milton," *Greyfriar*, 19 (1978), 7). It It may also be worth noting in this context that Henry Lawes referred to *Comus* as Milton's "off- spring" in the anonymous edition of 1637.

[10] Cf. the opening pun in Shakespeare's sonnet "The expense of spirit in a waste of shame."

[11] Why, however, the blind fury and not the blind fate? Milton was too good a classicist to be unaware that it was Atropos, not Megaera or one of her sisters, who held the fatal shears. No one, to the best of my knowledge, has yet offered a satisfactory explanation for this extraordinary conflation.

[12] See David Daiches, *Milton* (London: Hutchinson Univ. Library, 1957), p. 84.

[13] Lines 3-4. The association of "ears" with "shears" may be more than a matter of rhyme. William Prynne had recently had the former chopped off by the latter as Milton still remembered almost ten years later in his sonnet "On the New Forcers of Conscience."

[14] Donald M. Friedman comments on this episode: "The question he asks himself is not simply whether one kind of poetry is better than another, but whether the kind of poetry he knows to be better is worth pursuing if his labors and his achieved excellence are never to be given due praise" (p. 12). This, surely, is to read the answer back into the question. The swain says nothing about "achieved excellence" in lines 64ff. His concern is, rather, the possibility that he will never be given the opportunity to achieve the excellence his self-discipline deserves.

[15] "Orpheus" in *Dictionarium Historicum*.

NOTES TO CHAPTER SEVEN

[1] Indeed, in one respect Phoebus' speech is even more conclusive than Patience's: it ends with a couplet.

[2] Apollo's rebuke, in turn, reverses Priapus' comment in the first *Idyl*: "Wretched Daphnis, why doest thou pine away? The maiden is roaming among all the springs, all the groves... searching for thee" (82-85).

[3] The reference to the death of Hyacinth reminds us that Phoebus was a lover too. In addition to the obvious visual similarities between Camus and Silvanus there may also be a thematic connection. According to Ramus and Brinsley, Silvanus' *ferulas* came from "a kind of shrub or big herbe like unto fennel giant, with the branches whereof of schoole-masters used to iert children on the hands, whence came the name of Ferula" (Brinsley, p. 95, Ramus, p. 163). If there is any truth to Aubrey's story that Milton was beaten by his tutor, William Chappell, it is easy to see how such an etymology might have created a chain of association leading from Silvanus to the representative of Cambridge University.

4 See above, chapter 5.

5 Milton uses the same phrase to describe Samson's father, Manoa, in *Samson Agonistes*, 326. As we have just seen, Phoebus was generally believed to have been the father of King's mythic surrogate, Orpheus.

6 In addition to its usual meaning, "pledge" can also mean "child." See *Variorum*, p. 672.

7 Ralph Hone's attempt to prove that the Pilot is Christ rather than St. Peter is unpersuasive. See his article "The Pilot of the Galilean Lake," *SP*, 56 (1959), 55-61.

8 I assume with the editors of the *Variorum* that St. Peter's threat is directed not only at the wolves but also at the corrupt shepherds. Milton's phraseology implies a parallel between the Christian "engine" of retribution and the blind Fury's "abhorred shears."

9 Cf. Milton's *Nativity Ode*, 88-90.

10 Pan's "blood-hued elderberries" may have suggested Camus' "sanguine flower."

11 *Paraphrasis*, sig. M7ᵛ.

12 See below, note 29.

13 Cf. David Daiches' comment on the conclusion of Phoebus' speech in his *Milton*, p. 84.

14 "Approaches to *Lycidas*," p. 50.

15 The debate about the identity of the "two-handed engine" reveals the need to find in St. Peter's words some hope for a practical remedy in the here and now. For in addition to St. Michael's two-handed sword (which, I agree with Parker, is the strongest candidate) the other major contender has been what Milton was to call the "wholesome and preventive shears" of Parliament with its two houses.

16 'Paradiso' xxvii. 54-63, tr. Laurence Binyon.

17 C. H. Hereford, "Dante and Milton" in *The Post-War Mind of Germany* (Manchester: John Rylands Library), 1926; R. McKenzie, "Echoes of Dante in Milton's *Lycidas*," *Italica*, 20 (1943), 121-26.

18 See above, chapter 6.

19 Both the first *Idyl* and the tenth *Eclogue* conclude with a direct reference to the animals which the singer has in his care. Significantly, perhaps, there is no mention of the flock at the end of *Lycidas*.

20 Columbia, III, i, 242.

21 I have given my reasons for rejecting this assumption in my review of Hill's book in *R.E.S.*, ns. 31 (1981), 354-55.

22 I quote from the second draft of the letter in the *Trinity Manuscript*.

23 *Nativity Ode*, 28 and 133-40. In a number of respects, Milton's early

conception of the poet had more in common with the catholic than with the protestant notion of a priest. He was expected, for instance, to be chaste, and he served as a divinely appointed intermediary between God and man.

²⁴ "In Memory of W. B. Yeats," 36-37.

²⁵ See J. M. French, "The Digressions in Milton's *Lycidas*." From a psychological point of view, too, St. Peter's speech is thoroughly pertinent. In the face of the premature death of a young and promising human being, we naturally ask: why did it have to be him or her rather than someone else? In Lear's words, "Why should a dog, a horse, a rat have life, And thou no breath at all?" (V. iii. 306-07).

²⁶ "The Eclogue Tradition and the Nature of Pastoral," *College English*, 34 (1972), 353.

²⁷ "*Lycidas* and the Swain's Paideia." Friedman reads *Lycidas* in much the same way as Arthur Barker interpreted the *Nativity Ode*, as a record of the poet's conversion and self-dedication.

²⁸ Milton quotes Virgil's "hic gelidi fontes" in the *Epitaphium Damonis*, 71.

²⁹ Not for the first time, the poet has occupied the traditional position of his protagonist. See above, p. oo.

³⁰ For this reason, if for no other, it seems extremely unlikely that the dolphins which are summoned to waft Milton's "hapless youth" (164) could be related to the music-loving mammal which carried Arion to safety. As I have argued in *Notes and Queries*, ns. 25 (1978), 15-17, Milton was probably referring to the dolphins which bore the dead body of Hesiod back to shore.

NOTES TO CHAPTER EIGHT

¹ See D. C. Allen, *The Harmonious Vision* (Baltimore: Johns Hopkins Press, 1954), pp. 47-52.

² The legalistic language—"witness," "all-judging" (82)—implies the metaphor of a judicial proceeding.

³ Revelation, xiv. 2-4; xix. 6-7.

⁴ *Seriatim*: *Elegia Tertia*, 59-64; *At a Solemn Music*, 6-16; *Ad Patrem*, 30-37; *Epitaphium Damonis*, 212-17; *Reason of Church Government*, Columbia, III, i, 238; *Apology for Smectymnuus*, Columbia, III, i, 306.

⁵ *Reason of Church Government, loc. cit.*

⁶ *Loc. cit.*

⁷ One of the most influential Protestant commentators of the Renaissance, David Pareus, contended in his *Commentary Upon the Divine Revelation of the Apostle and Evangelist John*, trans. Elias Arnold (Amsterdam, 1644), that "this place serves neither to disgrace the marriage estate nor

to establish the merit of corporal virginity" (p. 334). For a detailed study of Puritan attitudes toward the interpretation of the Apocalypse see Michael Fixler, *Milton and the Kingdoms of God* (London: Faber & Faber, 1964); Austin C. Dobbins, *Milton and the Book of Revelation: The Heavenly Cycle* (University, Alabama: Univ. of Alabama Press, 1975).

[8] *The Apology* was published only a month or two before Milton's marriage.

[9] Quoted in Pareus, p. 334.

[10] Quoted in Edgar Wind, *Pagan Mysteries in the Renaissance* (London: Faber & Faber, 1968), p. 62. My italics.

[11] In the original Latin, Ficino and Milton use almost the same verb to describe the actions of the revellers: *debacchantur* (Ficino), *bacchantur* (Milton).

[12] "The Pattern of Milton's 'Nativity Ode'" in Alan Rudrum, *Milton, Modern Judgements* (London: Macmillan, 1968), p. 48.

[13] *Seriatim: The Shadow of Heaven* (Ithaca: Cornell Univ. Press, 1968), ch. 3; *John Milton* (New York: Columbia Univ. Press, 1963); "*Lycidas*: The Shattering of the Leaves," *SP*, 64 (1967), 51-64; "Flowerets and Sounding Seas: A Study in the Affective Structure of *Lycidas*" in Patrides, pp. 125-35; "Milton's Pastoral Monodies" in M. E. White, *Studies in Honor of Gilbert Norwood* (Toronto: Toronto Univ. Press, 1952).

[14] *Lycidas and the Italian Critics*, p. 128.

NOTES TO CHAPTER NINE

[1] "The Eclogue Tradition," p. 371. In similar vein Fish comments that the final lines are "perfectly, that is unrelievedly, conventional" ("*Lycidas*: A Poem Finally Anonymous," p. 16).

[2] "The Pastoral Elegy," p. 39.

[3] *Complete Poems and Major Prose*, p. 125. Cf. Ralph W. Condee's comment in *Structure in Milton's Poetry* (University Park Pennsylvania: Pennsylvania State Univ. Press, 1974), p. 39: "The whole passage parallels the conclusion of Virgil's tenth eclogue, which sings the sorrow of Gallus," and Eric Smith, p. 138.

[4] "Essays in Analysis," p. 151. The assymetry of the ending is not always recognized, however. For instance, in his essay on "Milton's Pastoral Monodies," A. S. P. Woodhouse writes: "*Lycidas* commences with a Prelude which is part of the monody but which is to be balanced by the brief Epilogue, so that together they give something of the effect of the traditional framework setting" (p. 273). A. E. Barker's famous analysis of the tripartite nature of the poem also implies that the epilogue is

balanced by a prologue, as does the widespread use of the word "framing" to describe the conclusion of *Lycidas*.

[5] "A Poem Nearly Anonymous," *American Review*, 4 (1933), reprinted in Patrides, pp. 64-81.

[6] "John Crowe Ransom and *Lycidas*, a Reappraisal," *College English*, 17 (1956), 227.

[7] Clay Hunt argues that Milton employs the term in the sense it had come to have in the new music of the period, that is, "a musical declamation *in stilo recitativo* for a solo voice" (p. 163). In either case, the dramatic character of the monody is still its dominant feature.

[8] The distinctiveness of Milton's final stanza emerges even more clearly if we compare it with its other major analogue, the conclusion of Canto vi of Phineas Fletcher's *Purple Island*:

> But see, the stealing night with softly pace
> To flie the western sunne, creeps up the east;
> Cold Hesper 'gins unmask his evening face;
> And calls the winking starres from drouzie rest:
> Home then my lambes; the falling drops eschew:
> To morrow shal ye feast in pastures new,
> And with the rising sunne banquet on pearled dew.

After pointing out the obvious parallels in theme and phraseology, G. S. Fraser remarks that "the most surprising resemblance is a much broader one; the tone, mood, and pace of Fletcher's passage are very like Milton, and indeed one would have said...typically Miltonic" ("Approaches to *Lycidas*," p. 37). The overall effect, however, is the exact converse. Fletcher's stanza is a dramatic interval in a narrative poem; Milton's is a narrative epilogue to a dramatic poem.

[9] "Five Types of *Lycidas*" in Patrides, p. 222.

[10] *By Mourning Tongues*, p. 27.

[11] W. B. Madsen, "The Voice of Michael in *Lycidas*," SEL 3 (1963), 1-7.

[12] *Baroque Lyric Poetry* (New Haven: Yale Univ. Press, 1961), p. 151.

[13] *Seriatim*: "The Ghost of Milton" in *The Common Asphodel* (London: Hamish Hamilton, 1949), pp. 322-23; *John Milton* (London: Longman's, Green & Co., 1960), pp. 48-49; *Milton* (London: Chatto & Windus, 1930), pp. 79-85.

[14] See above, p. 000.

[15] *Poetic Closure* (Chicago: Univ. of Chicago Press, 1968), p. 194, n. 55.

[16] *Op. cit.*, p. 5.

[17] *Inwrought with Figures Dim* (The Hague: Mouton, 1974), p. 12.

[18] *Ibid.*, pp. 31-32.

[19] *Op. cit.*, p. 8.

20 *Op. cit.*, p. 145.

21 *Op. cit.*, p. 71.

22 Fish, p. 2.

23 "Who is Lycidas?", p. 187.

24 *Op. cit.*, p. 8.

25 *Op. cit.*, p. 11.

26 *Loc. cit.* Curiously enough, F. T. Prince does not mention this aspect of the question in his study *The Italian Element in Milton's Verse* (Oxford: Clarendon Press, 1954). The basic verse pattern of *Lycidas*, he argues, is an adaptation of the Italian *canzone*, which he defines as "a complex fully rhymed stanza of some length, repeated several times, and followed by a short concluding stanza, the *commiato*." The final *ottava rima*, he believes, "undoubtedly corresponds in its own way to a *commiato*" (pp. 72-73, 120). But a *commiato* rarely, if ever, had the rhyme scheme of an *ottava rima*—the example Prince cites from Guarini's *Pastor Fido*, for instance, is in rhyming couplets.

27 Indeed, Tasso argues in his dialogue, *La Cavaletta*, that the *ottava rima*, being regular, is "less suited to lamentation" than less regular forms (Quoted in Hunt, p. 119).

28 *John Milton: Poet, Priest and Prophet* (London: Macmillan, 1979), p. 68.

29 *Visionary Poetics*, p. 81.

30 *The Reason of Church Government*, Columbia, III, i, 234.

31 *Ibid.*, p. 241.

32 I cannot agree, however, with Lambert when she associates Milton's "fresh woods" with Dante's "dark wood of experience" (p. 181). The conclusion of *Lycidas* seems to me much more open-ended and less claustrophobic than that phrase implies. The final lines of *Paradise Lost* come closer in feeling.

33 Columbia, XII, 27. Milton uses the same image in *Ad Salsillum*, 9-11, to to describe his departure for Italy.